THANK YOU
FOR PURCHASE IT
IT REALLY MEANS
A LOT TO US !

PLEASE SHARE YOUR EXPERIENCE ON THE AMAZON!!!

We hope you have an amazing coloring journey with this book, and we appreciate your feedback to help us develop and deliver more amazing drawings to our audience, and to assist future purchasers in making confident choices.

Scan me !

ABOUT THE AUTHOR

WELCOME TO COLODEN, WHERE WE SPECIALIZE IN CREATING UNIQUE AND CAPTIVATING COLORING BOOKS FOR ADULTS AND CHILDREN ALIKE. OUR MISSION IS TO PROVIDE A CREATIVE OUTLET FOR PEOPLE OF ALL AGES TO EXPRESS THEMSELVES THROUGH THE JOY OF COLORING. WE BELIEVE THAT COLORING IS NOT JUST A FUN ACTIVITY, BUT ALSO A THERAPEUTIC ONE THAT CAN REDUCE STRESS AND PROMOTE MINDFULNESS.

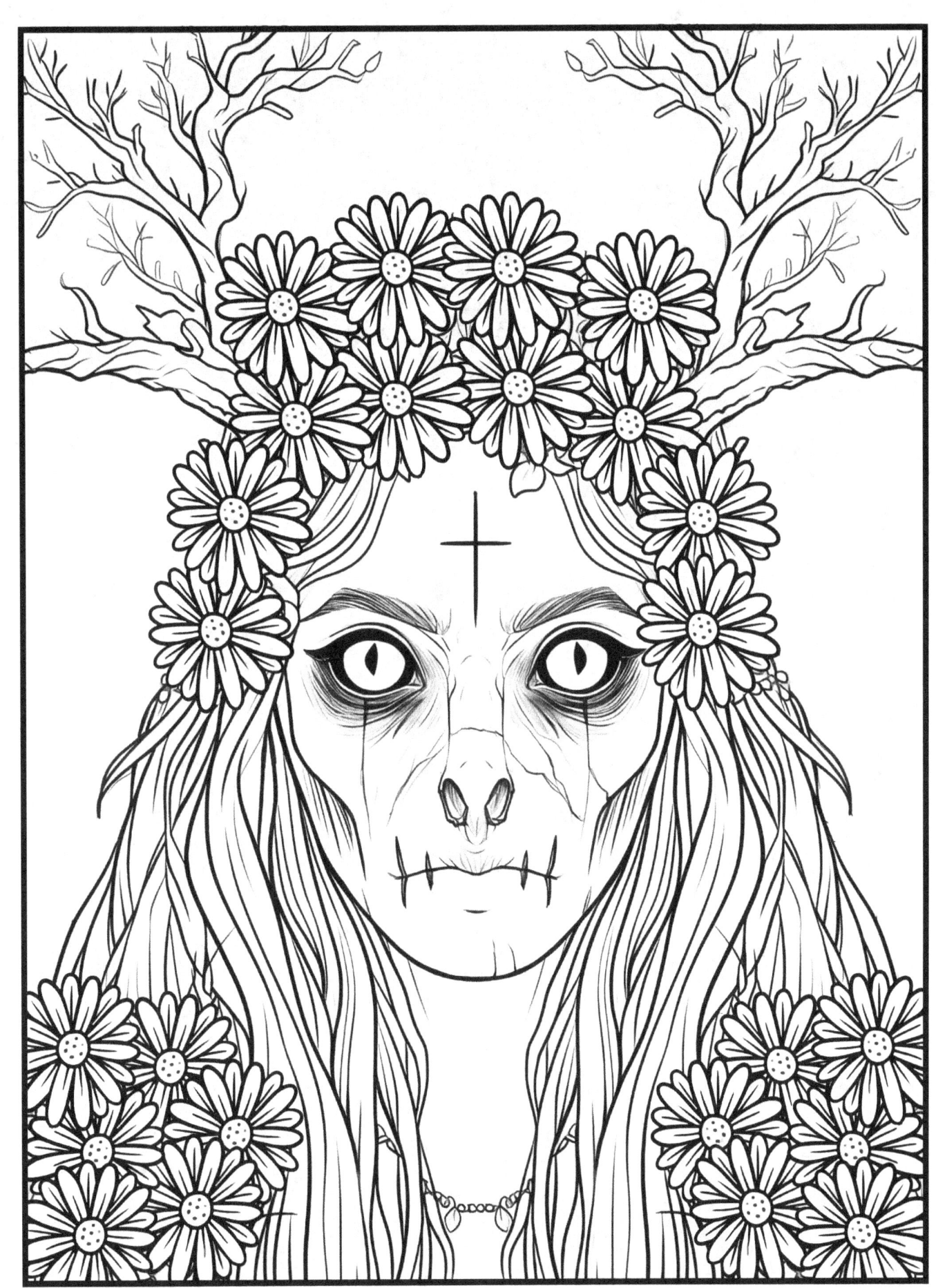

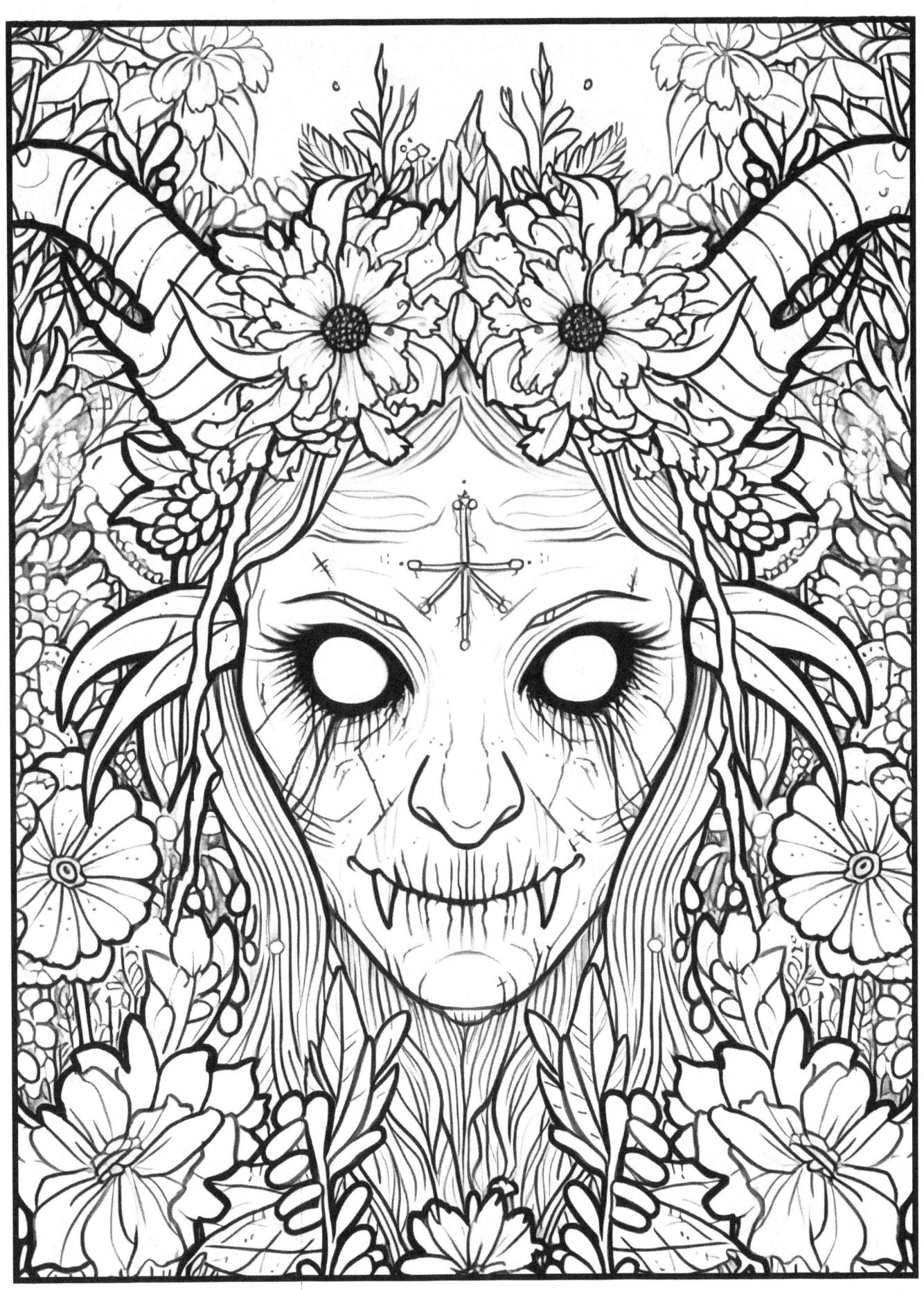

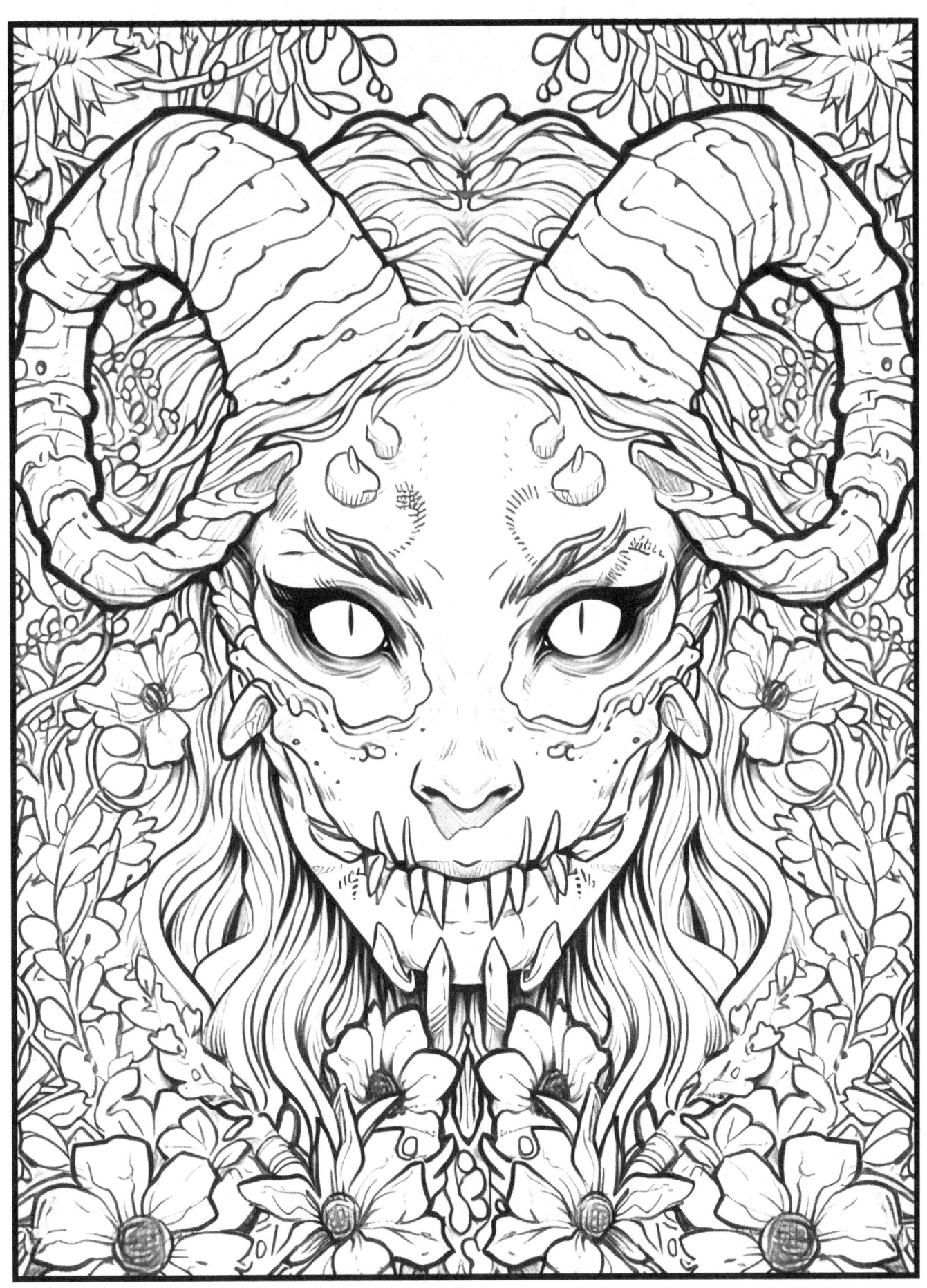

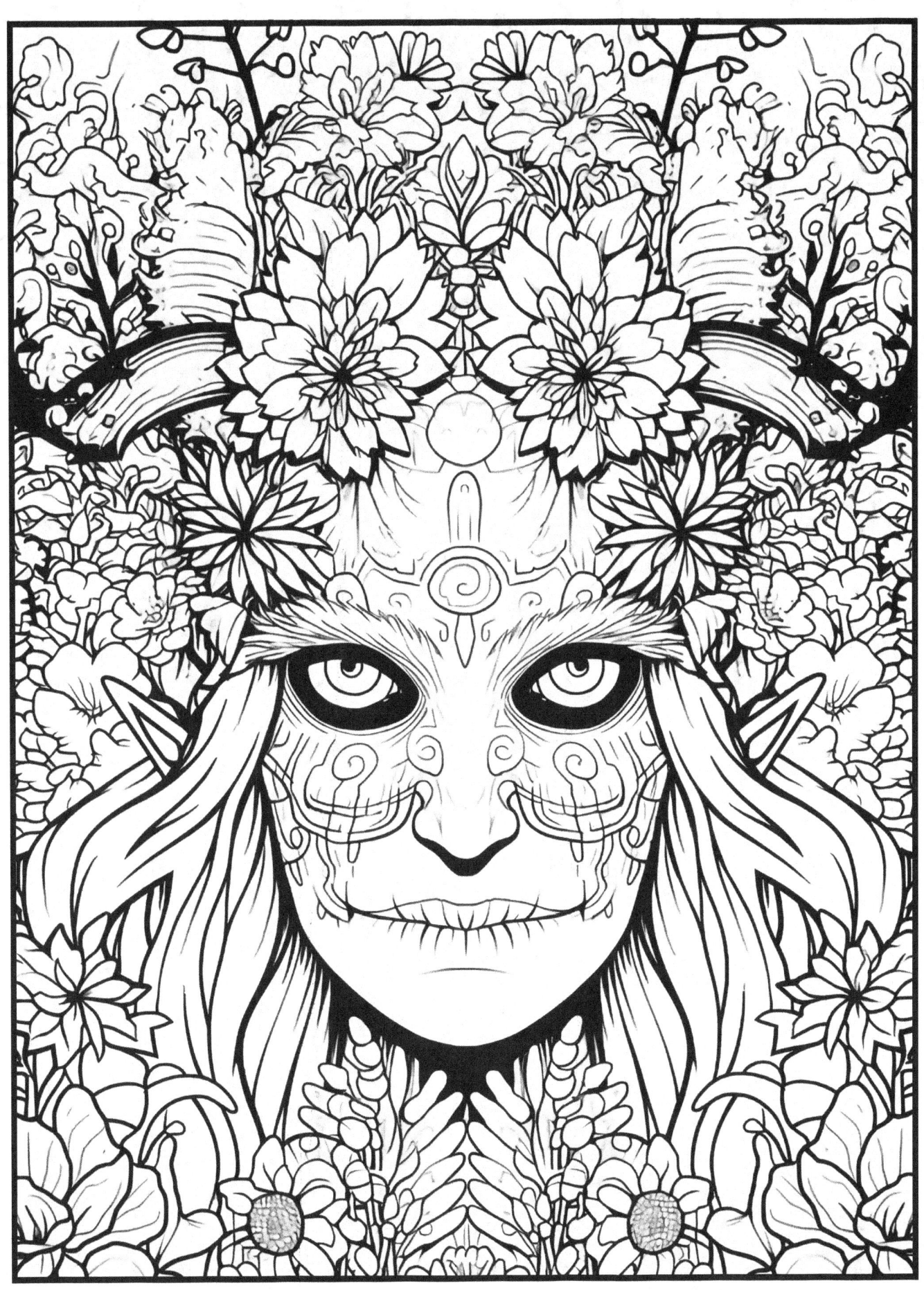

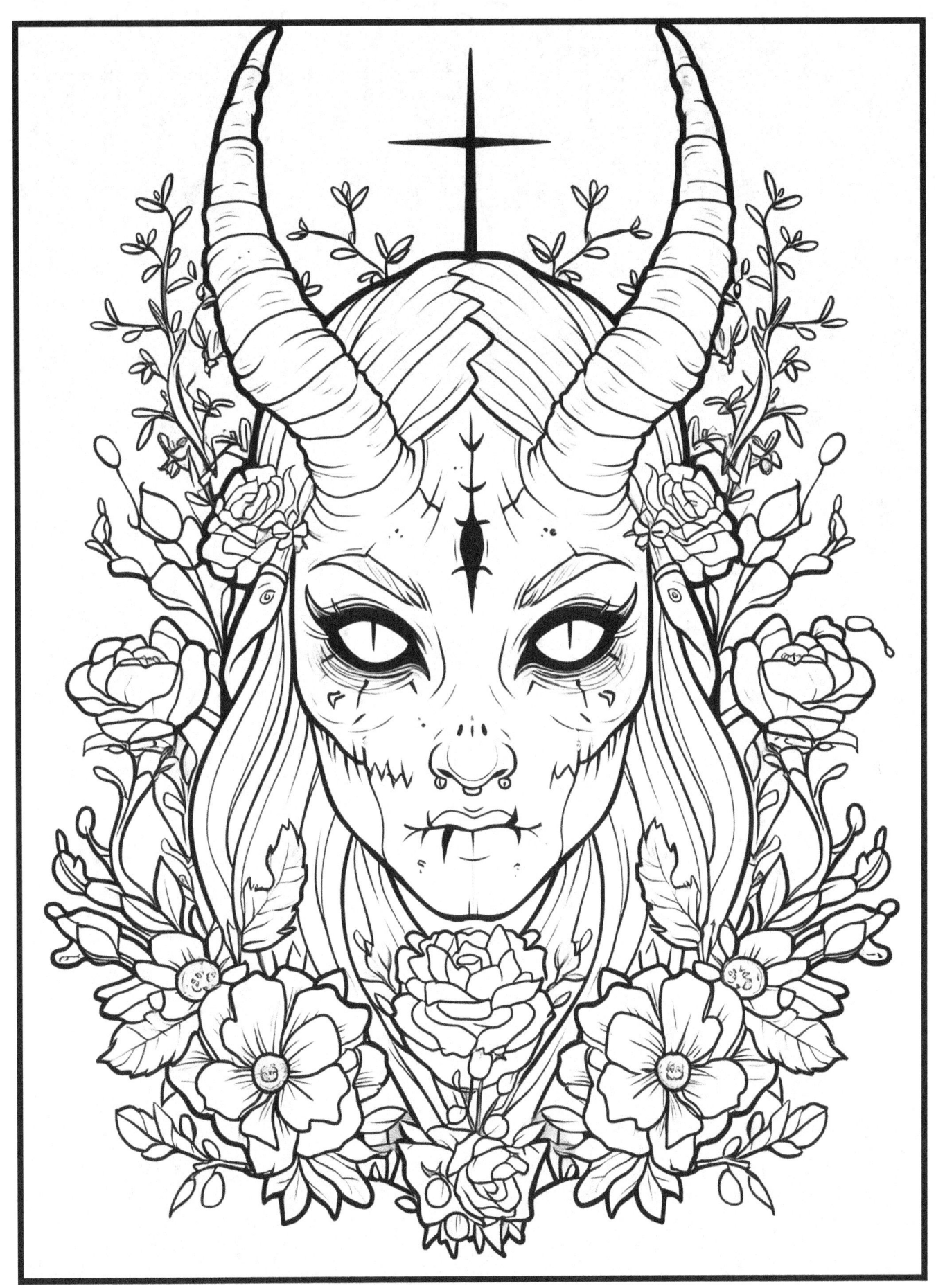

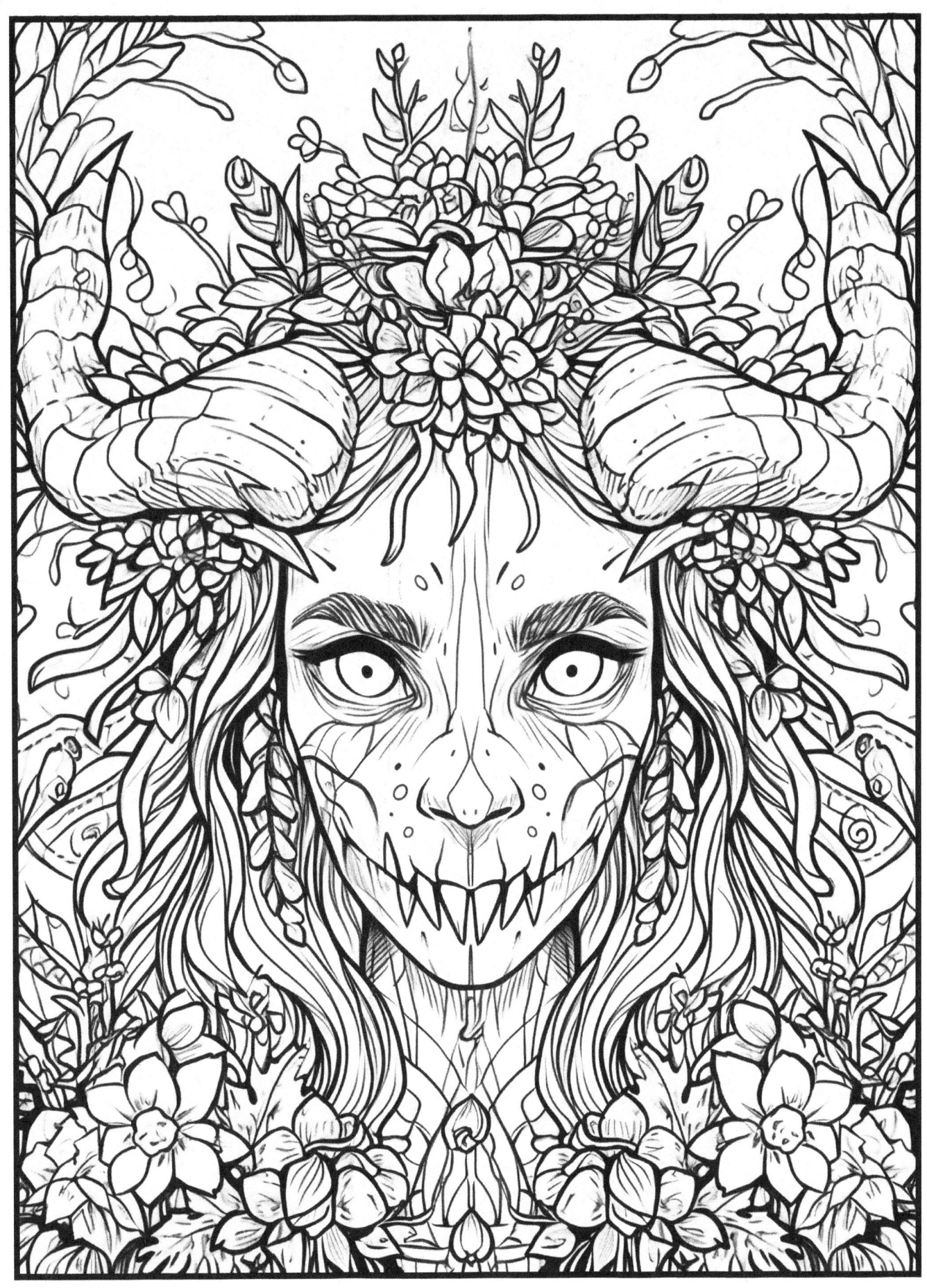

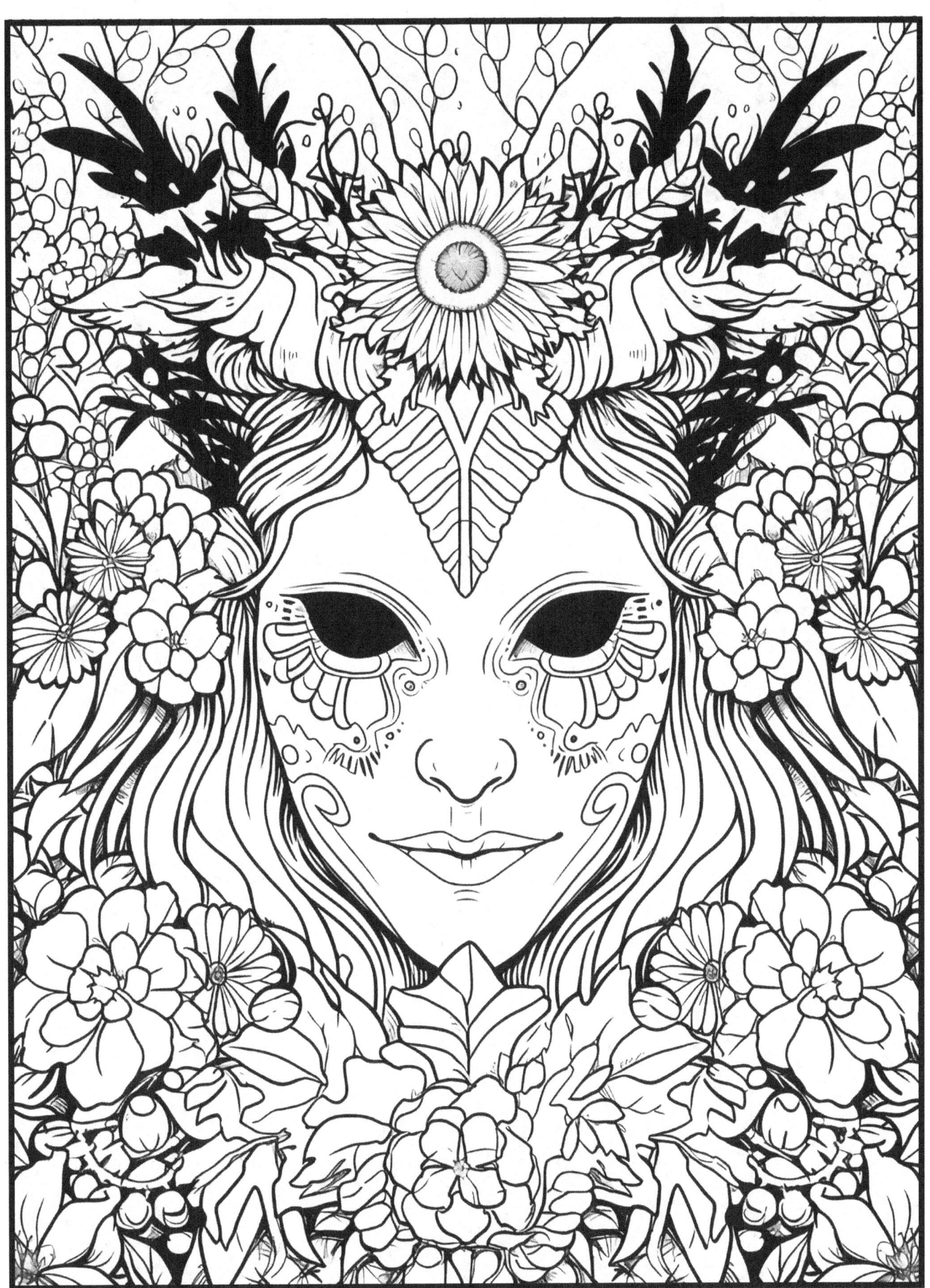

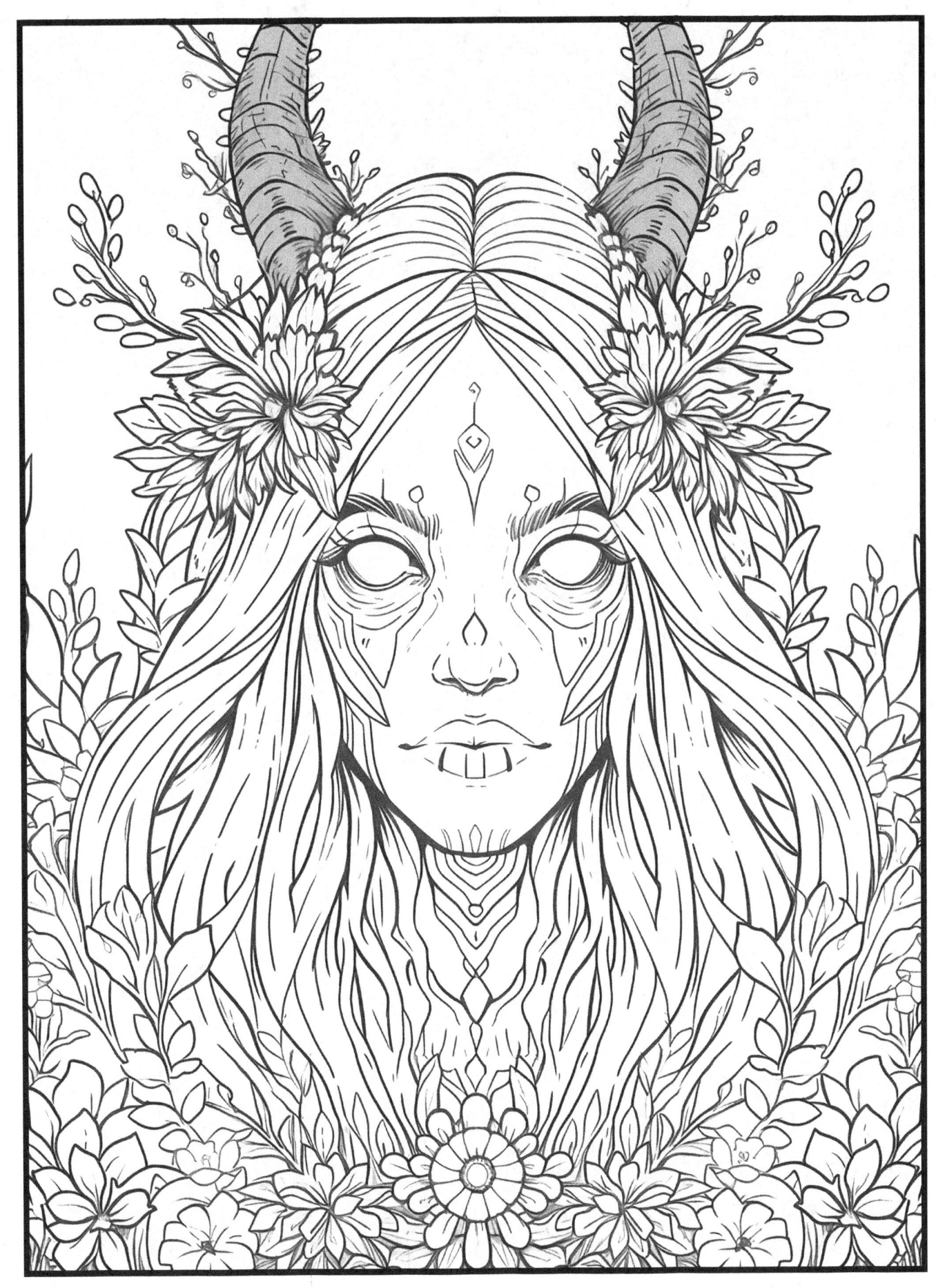

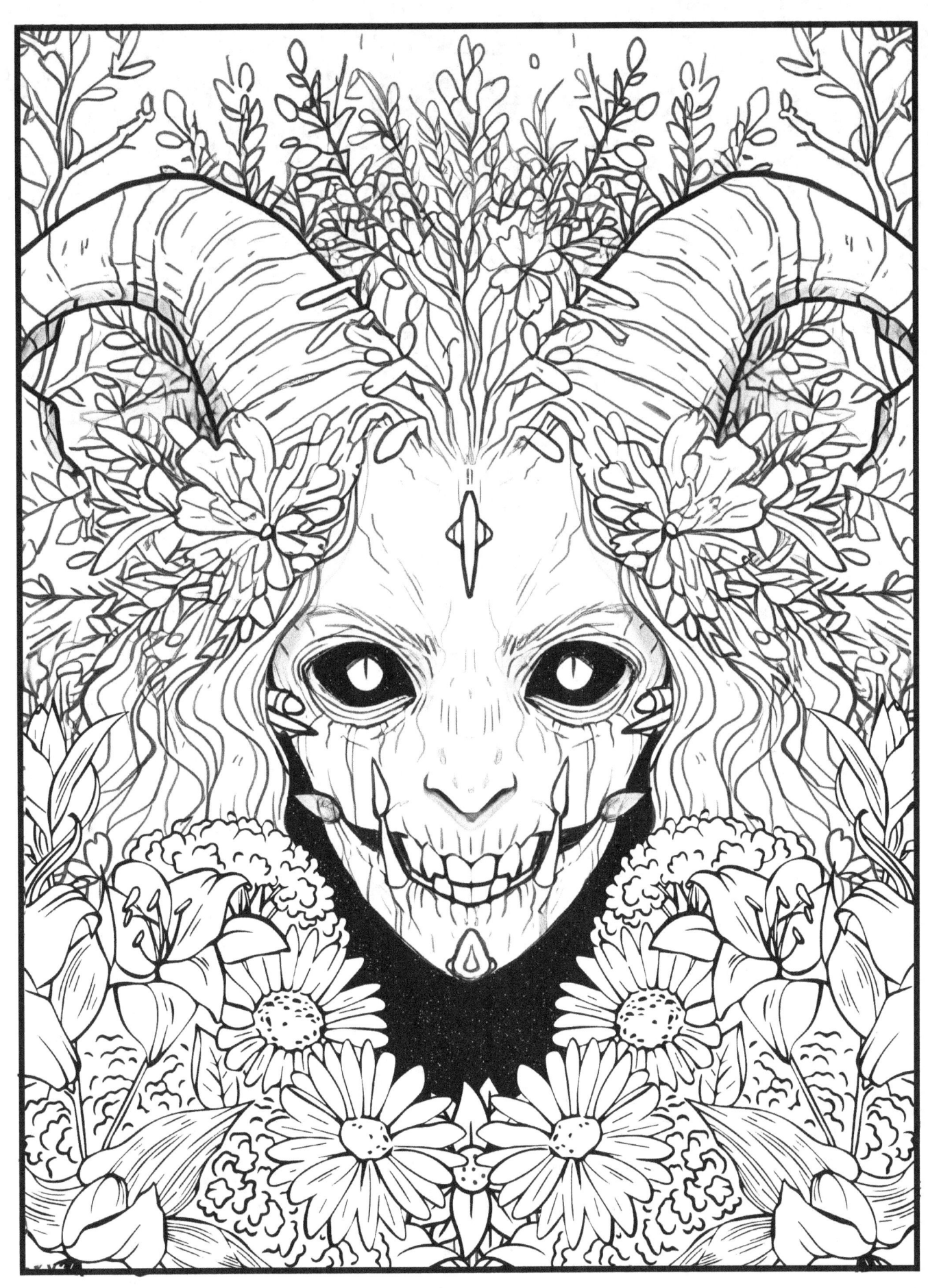

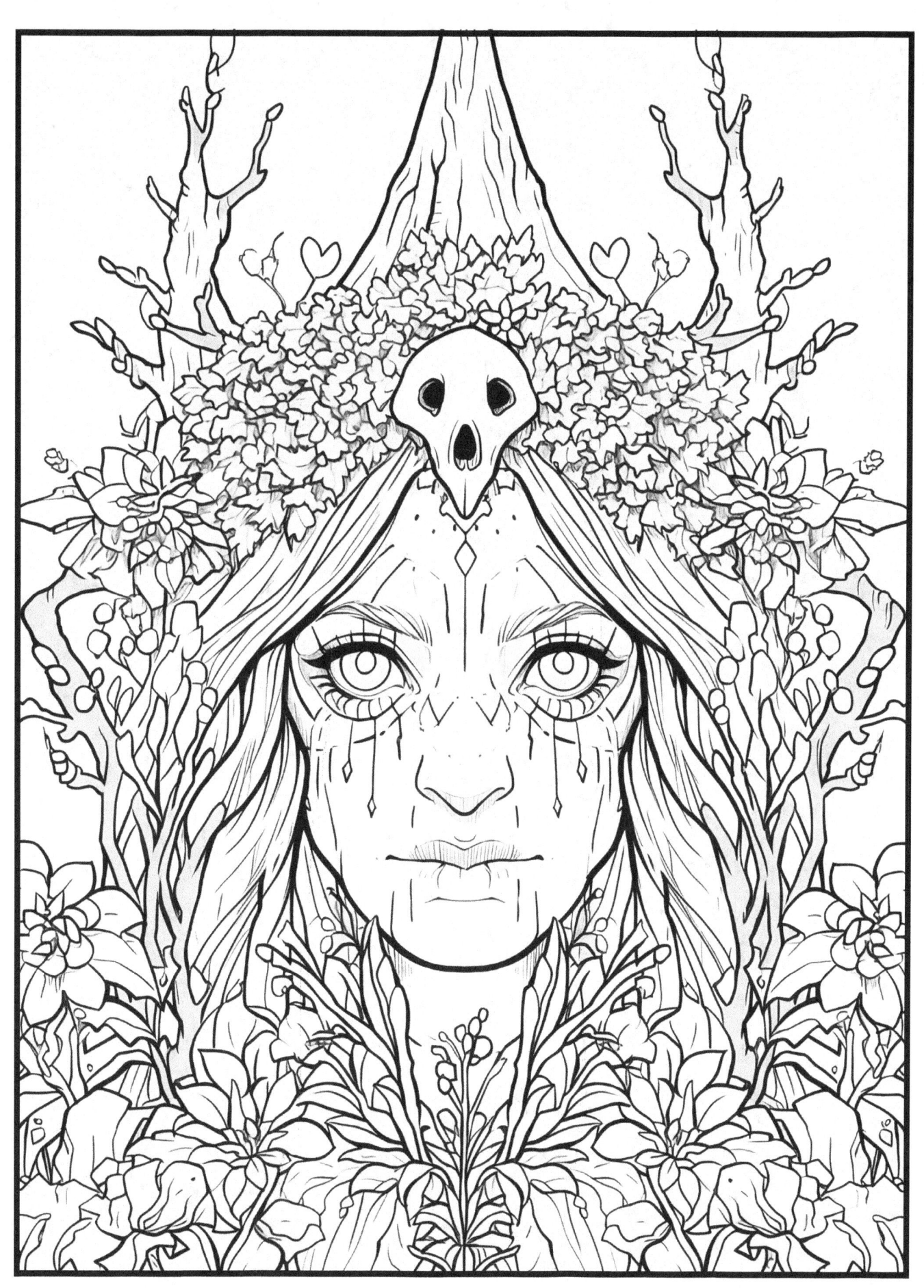

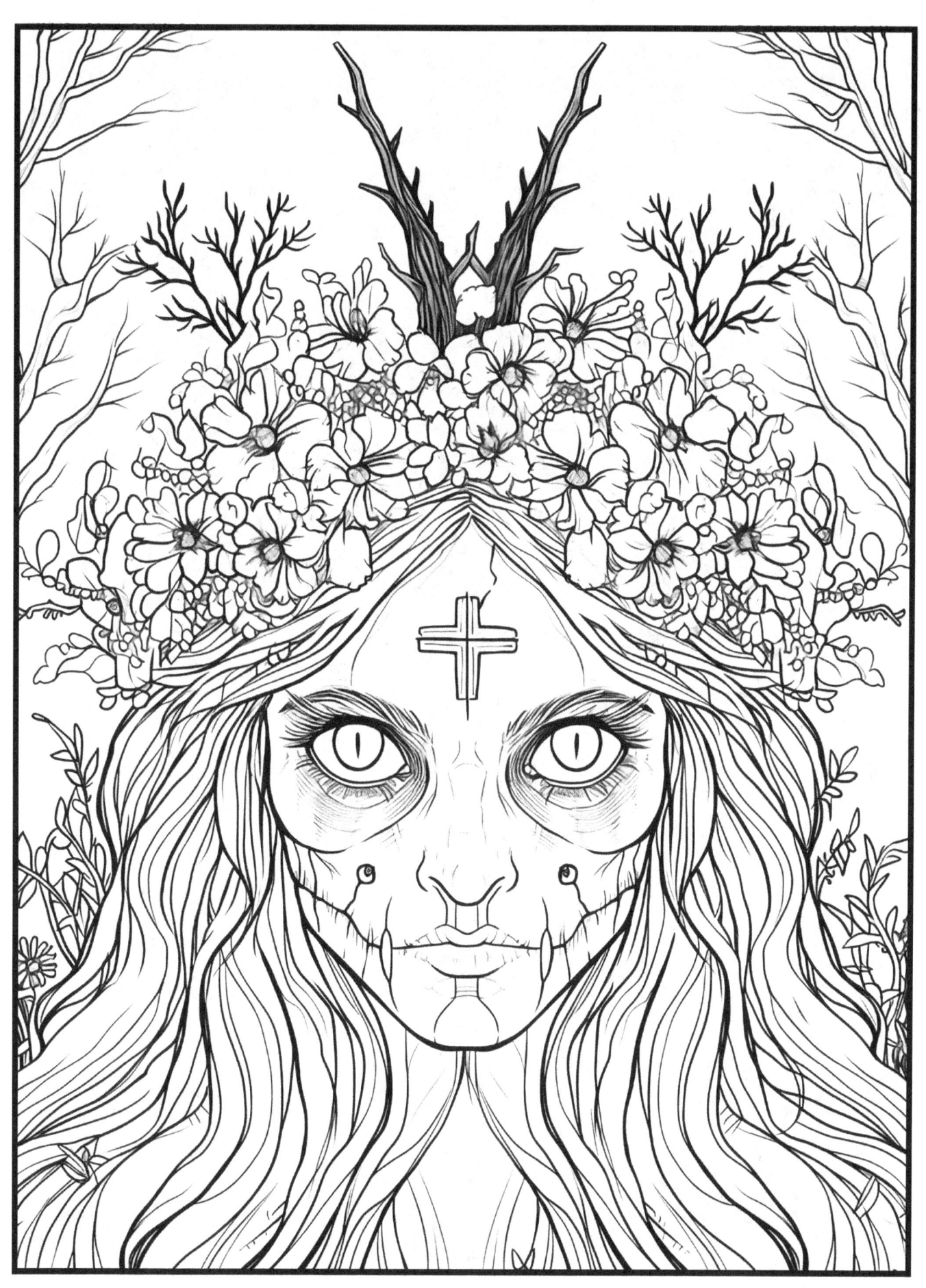

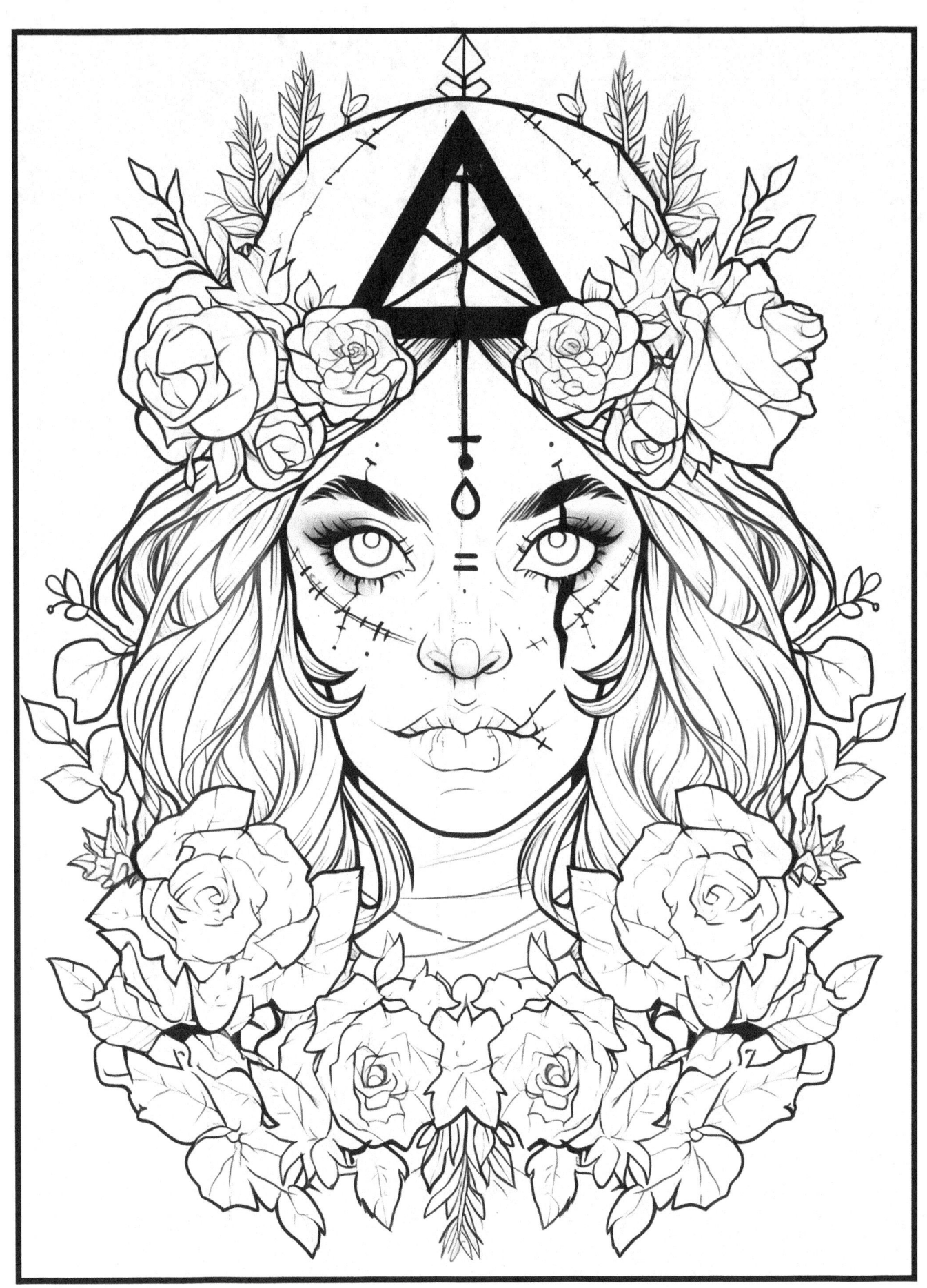

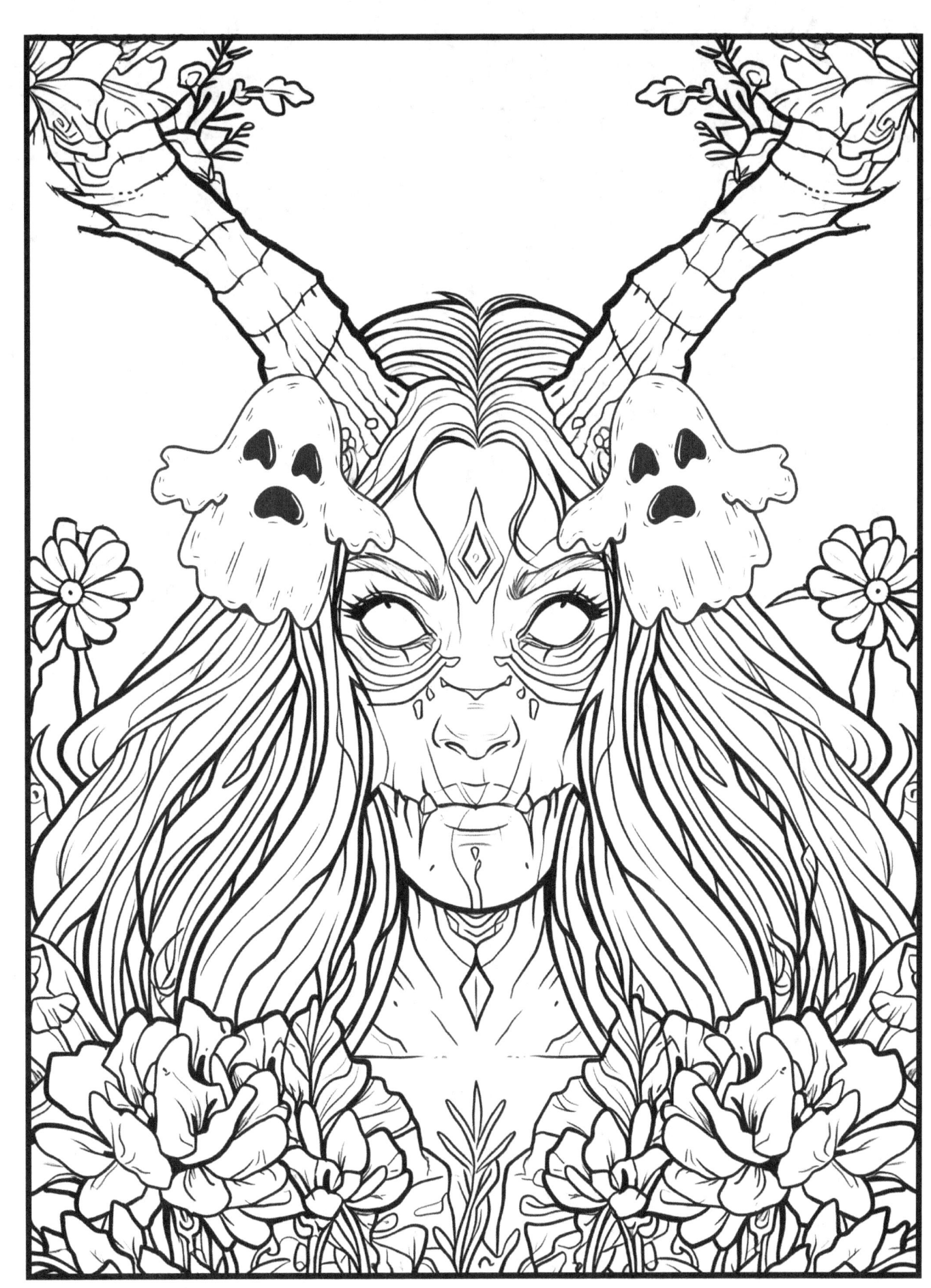

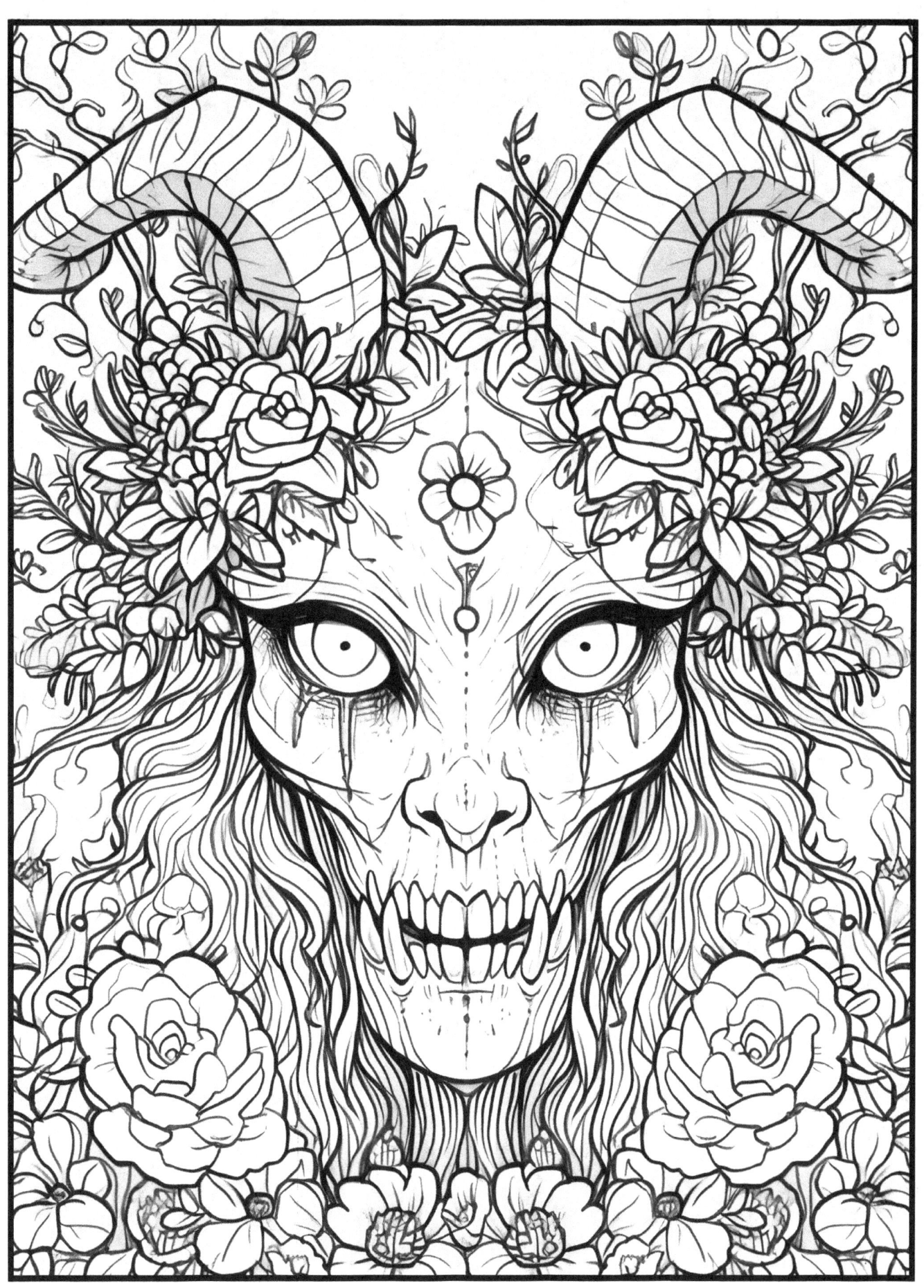

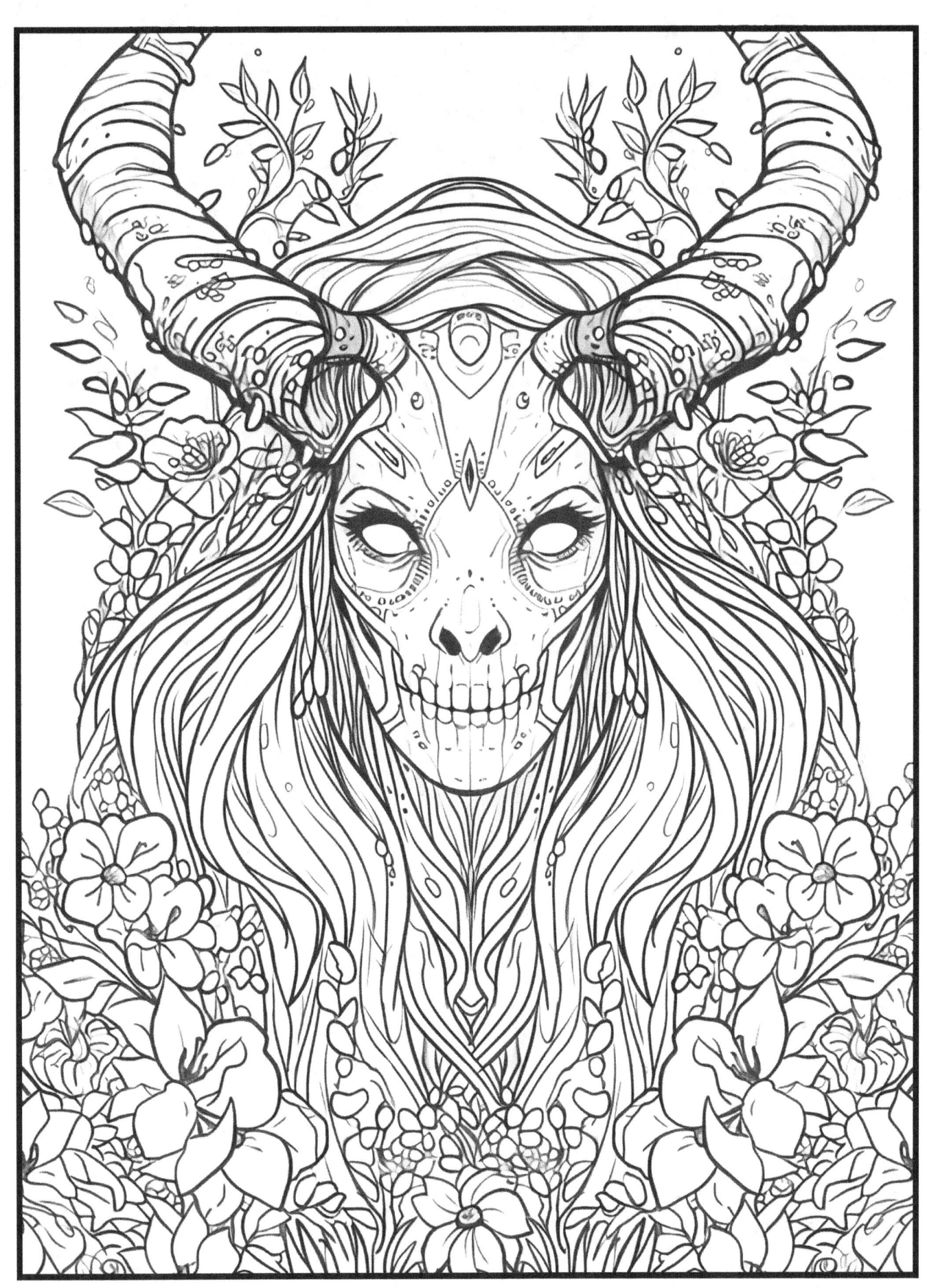

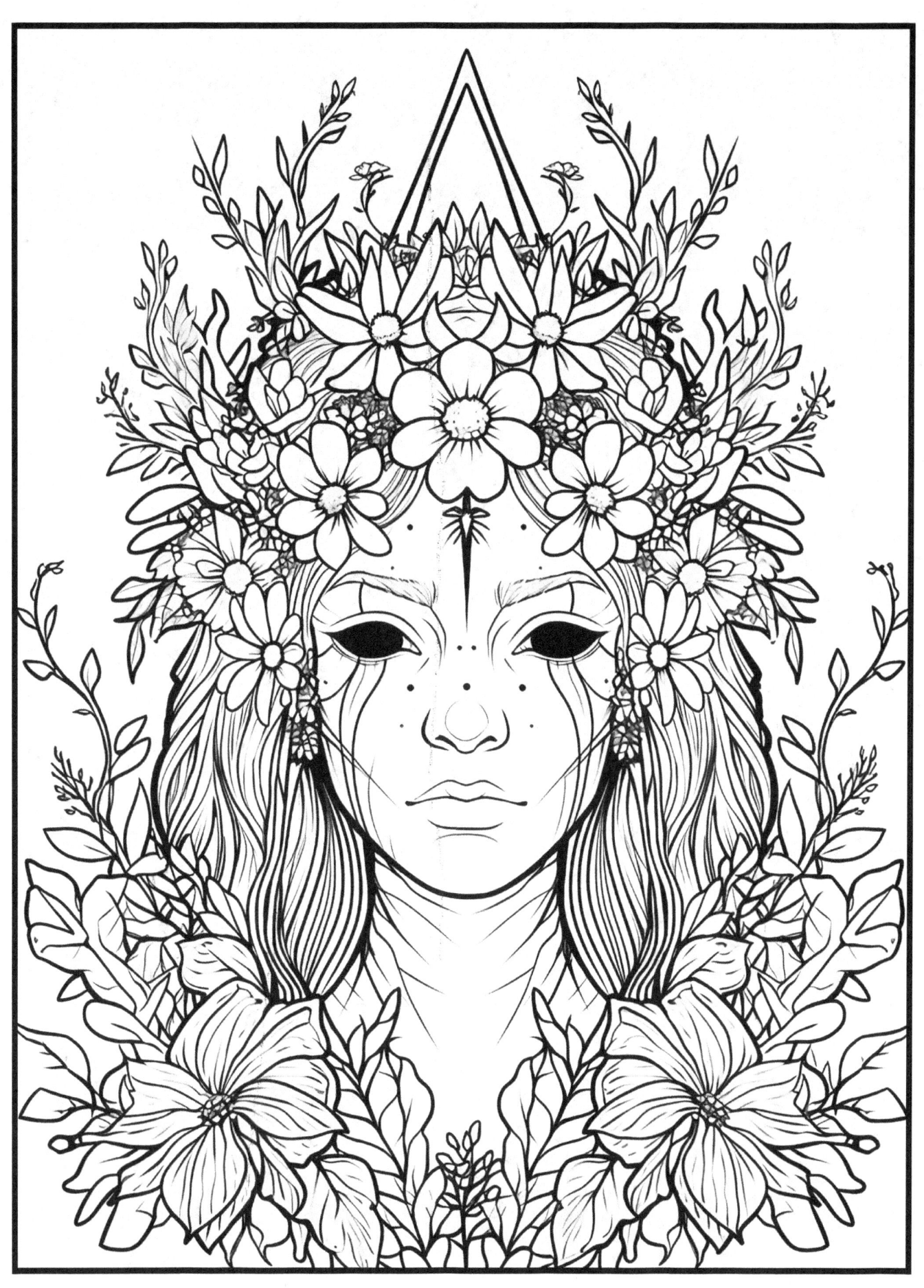

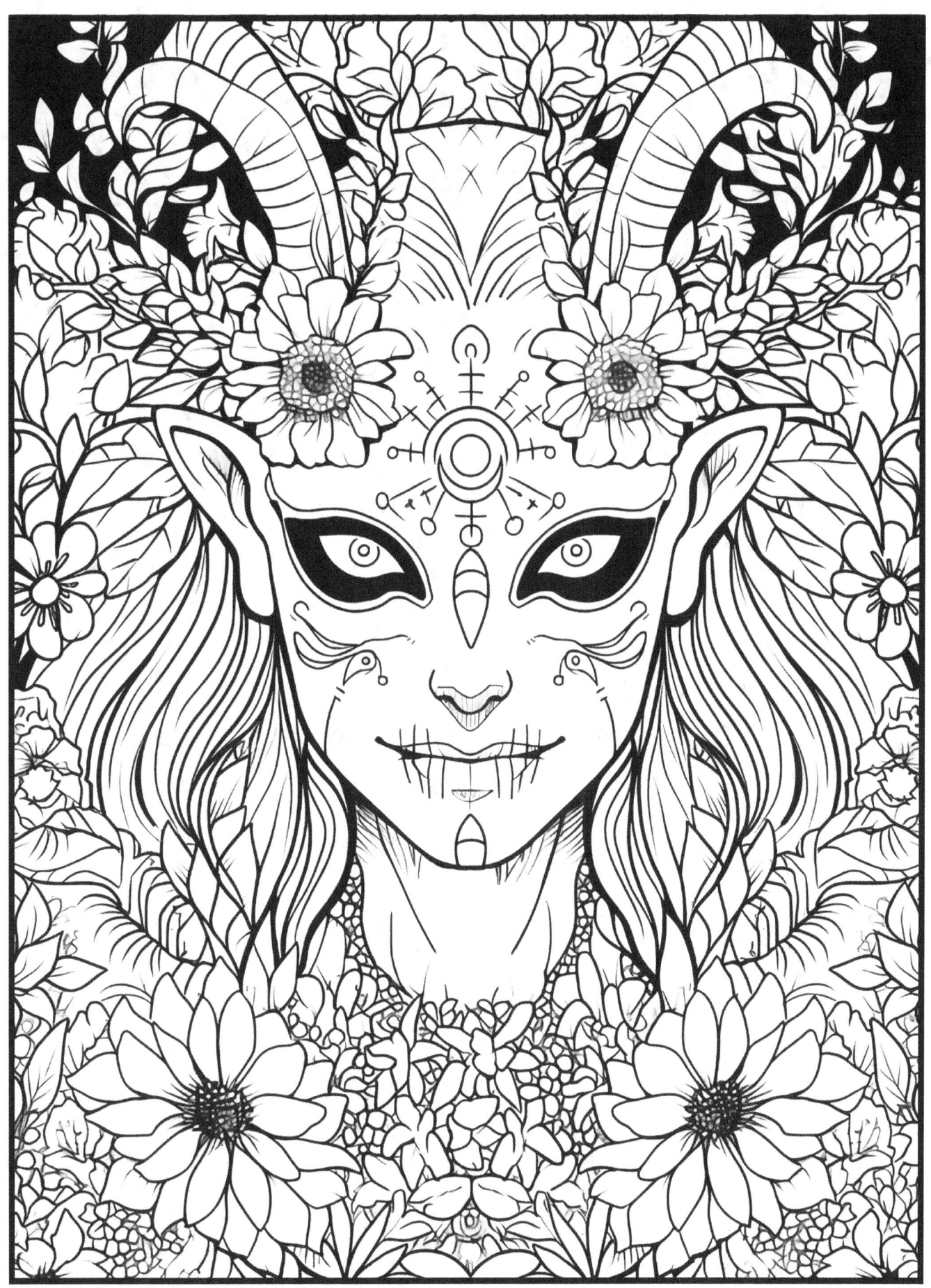

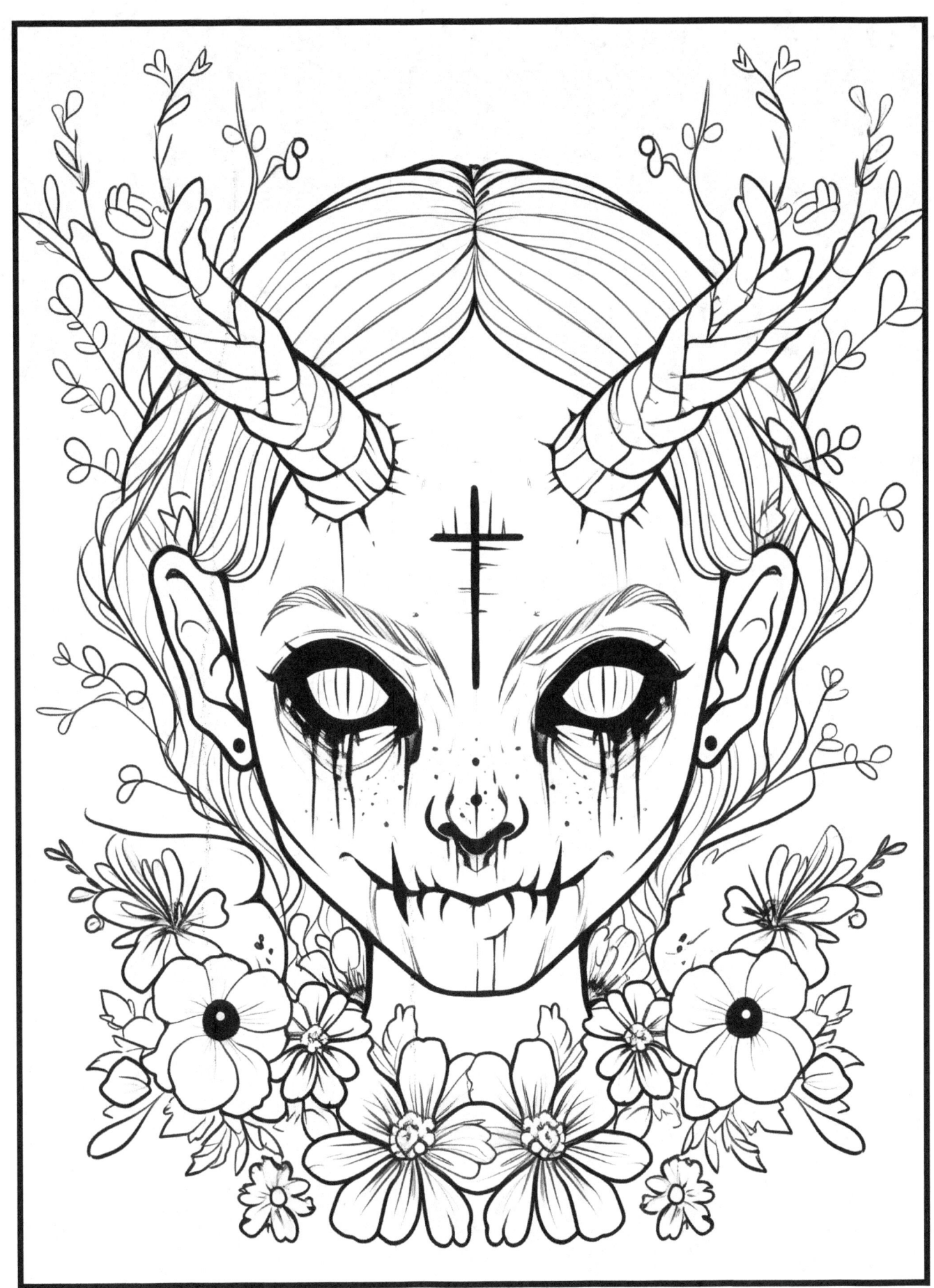

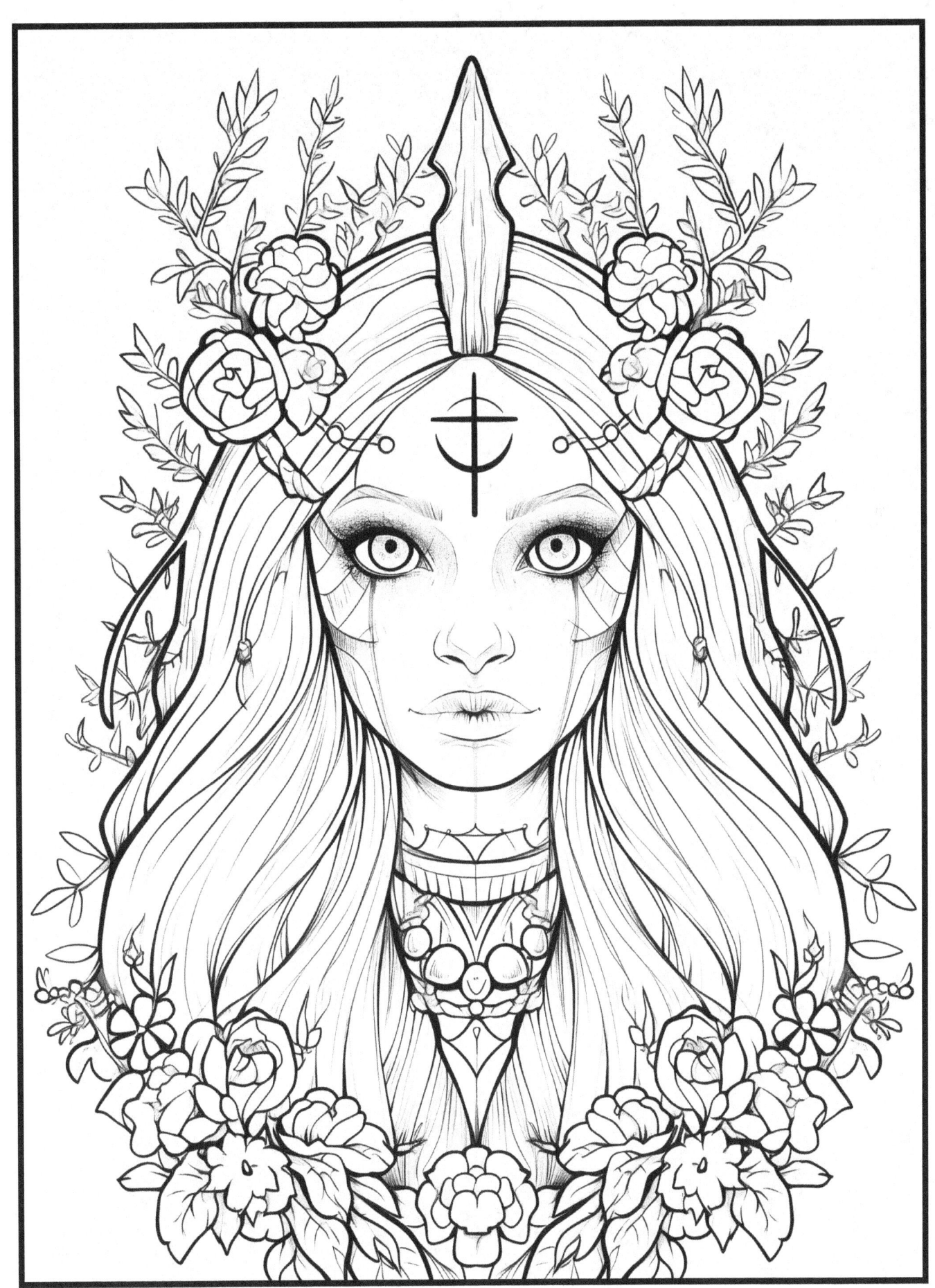

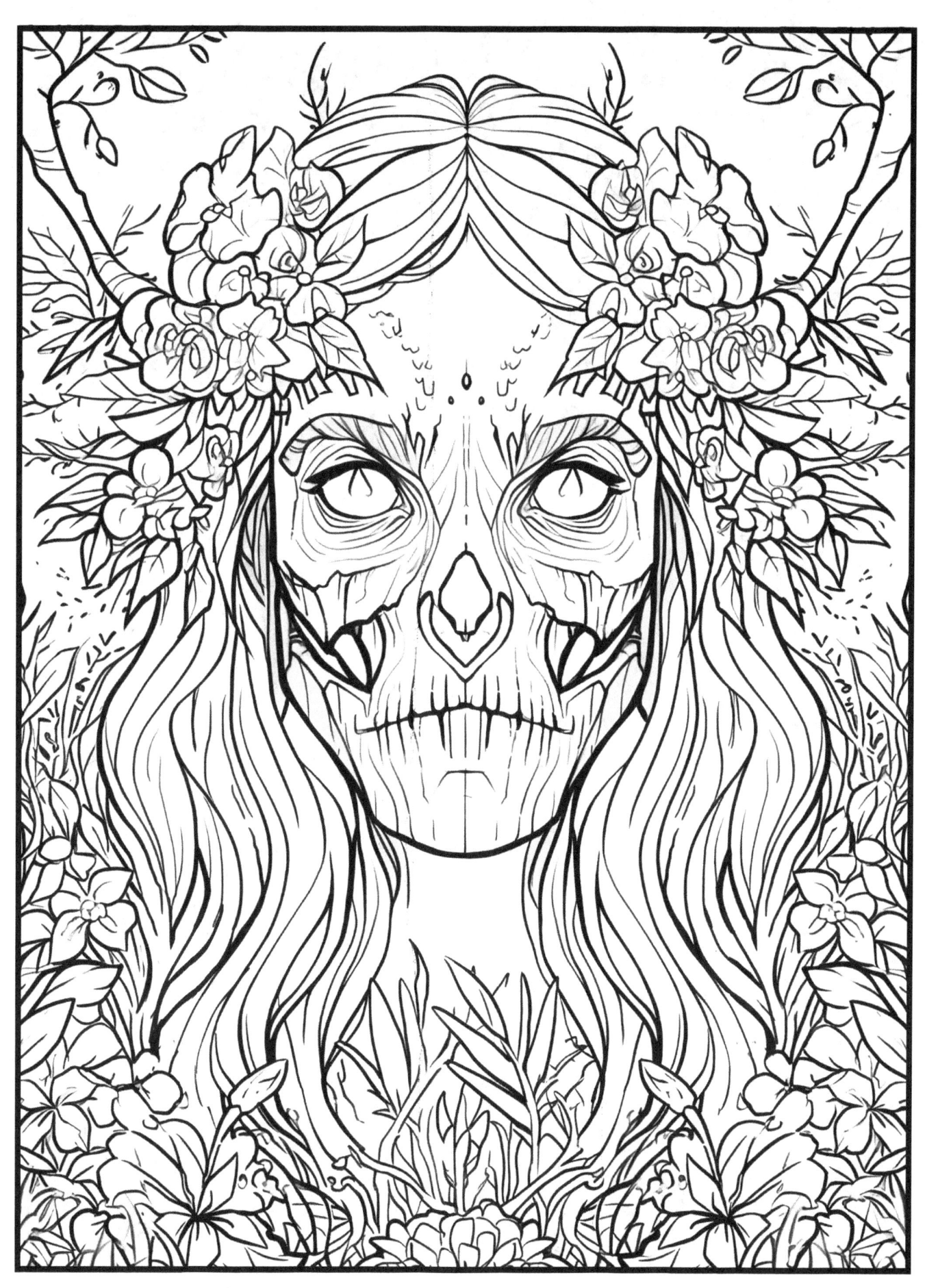

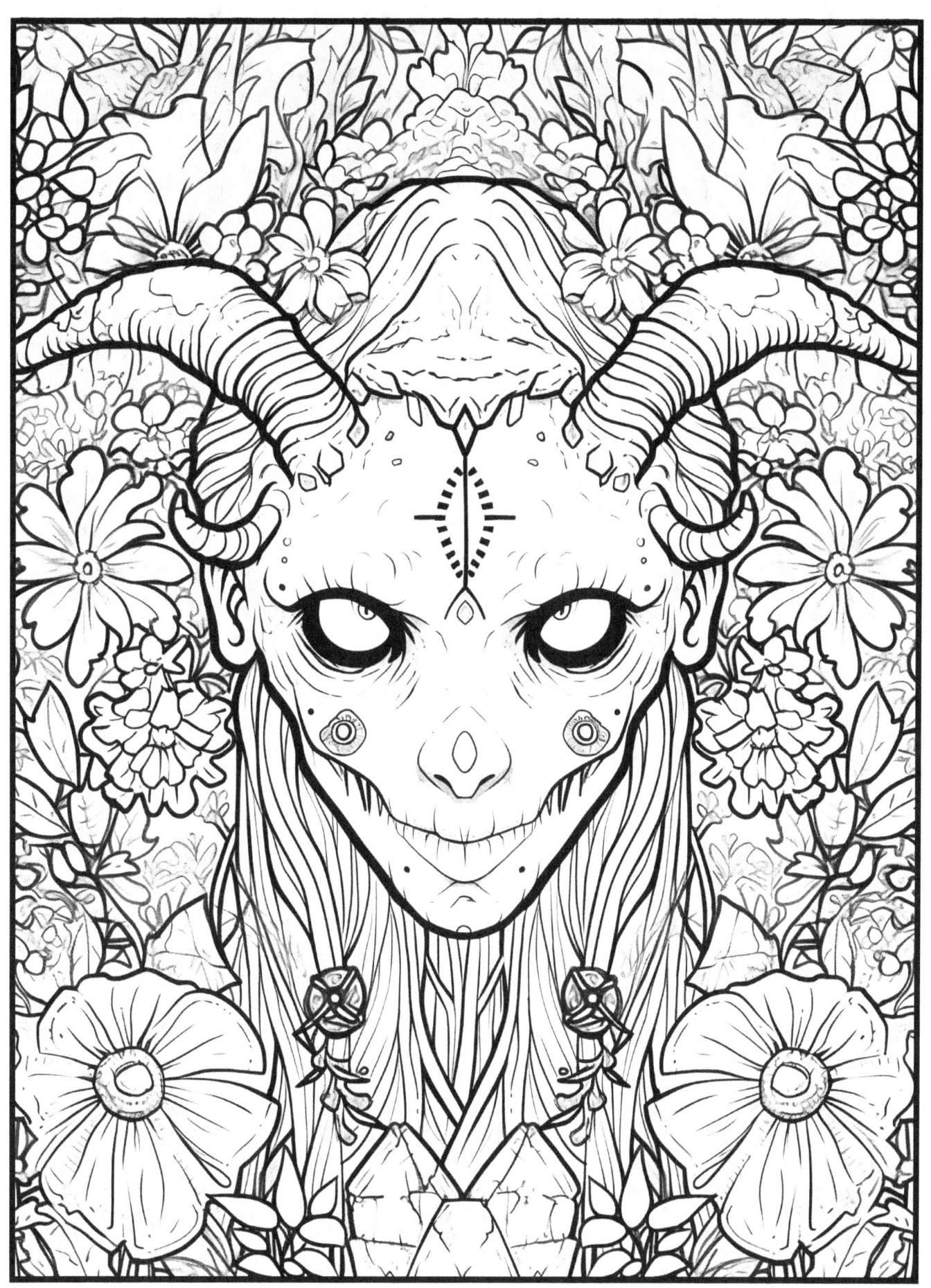

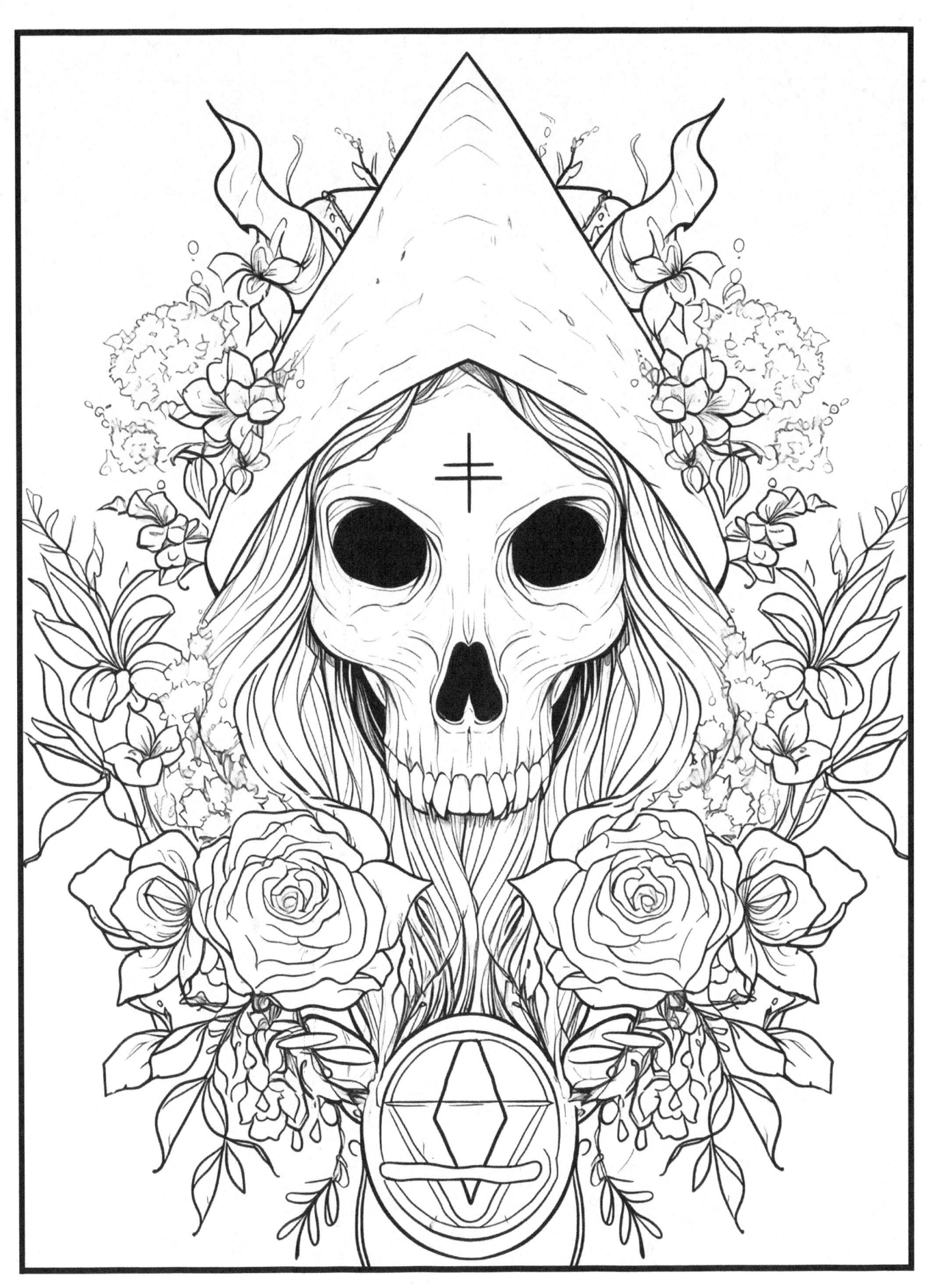

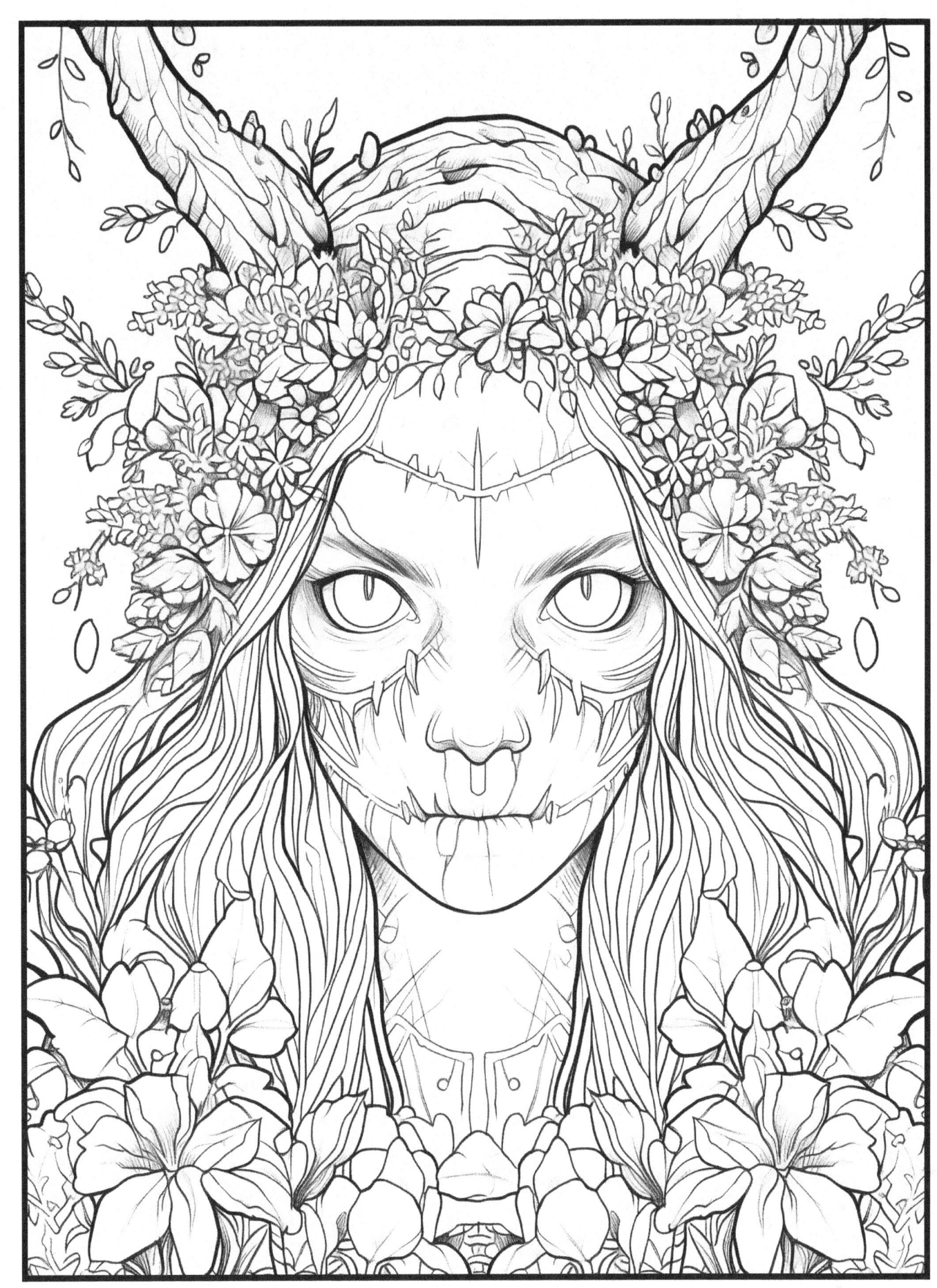

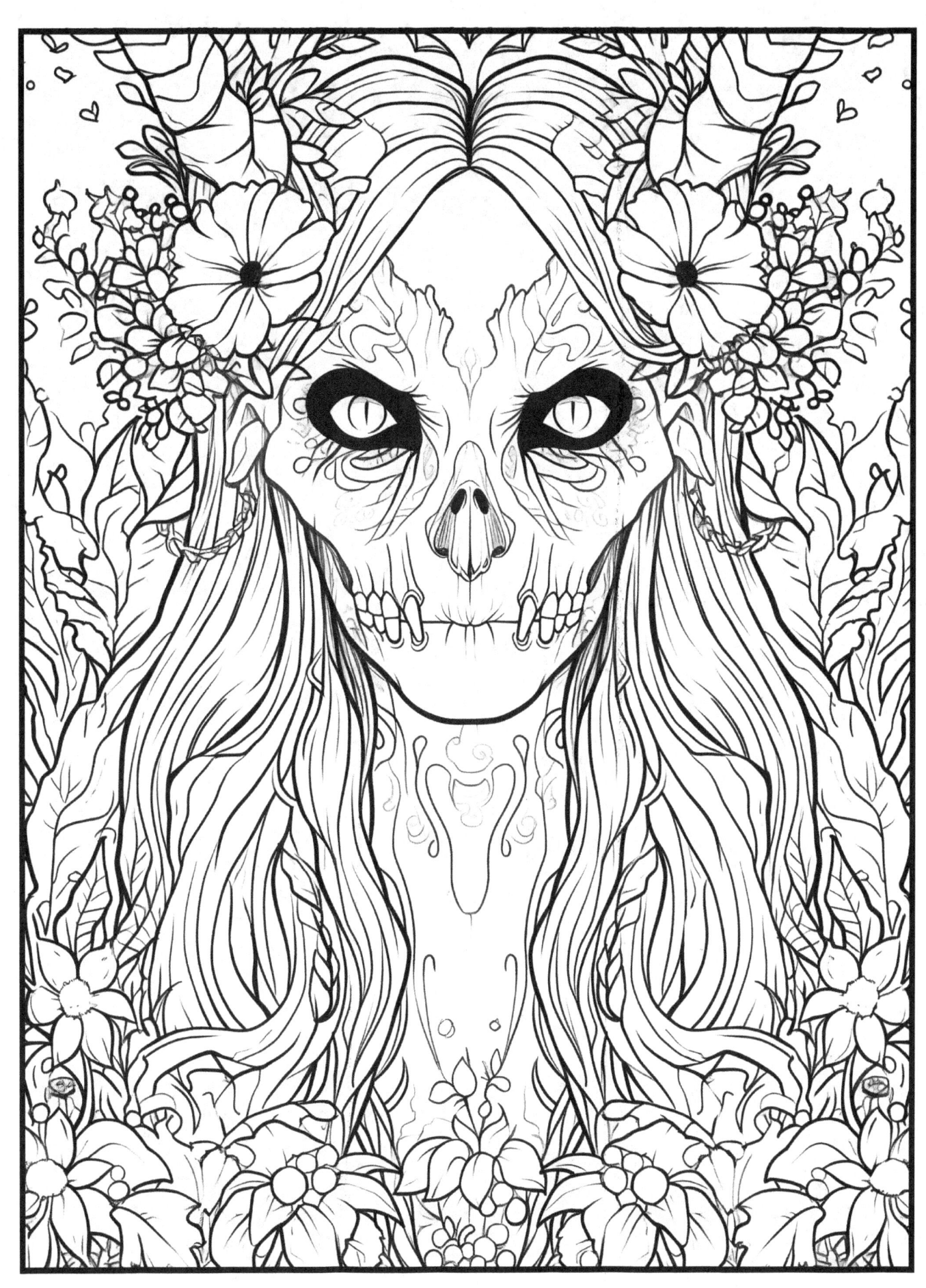

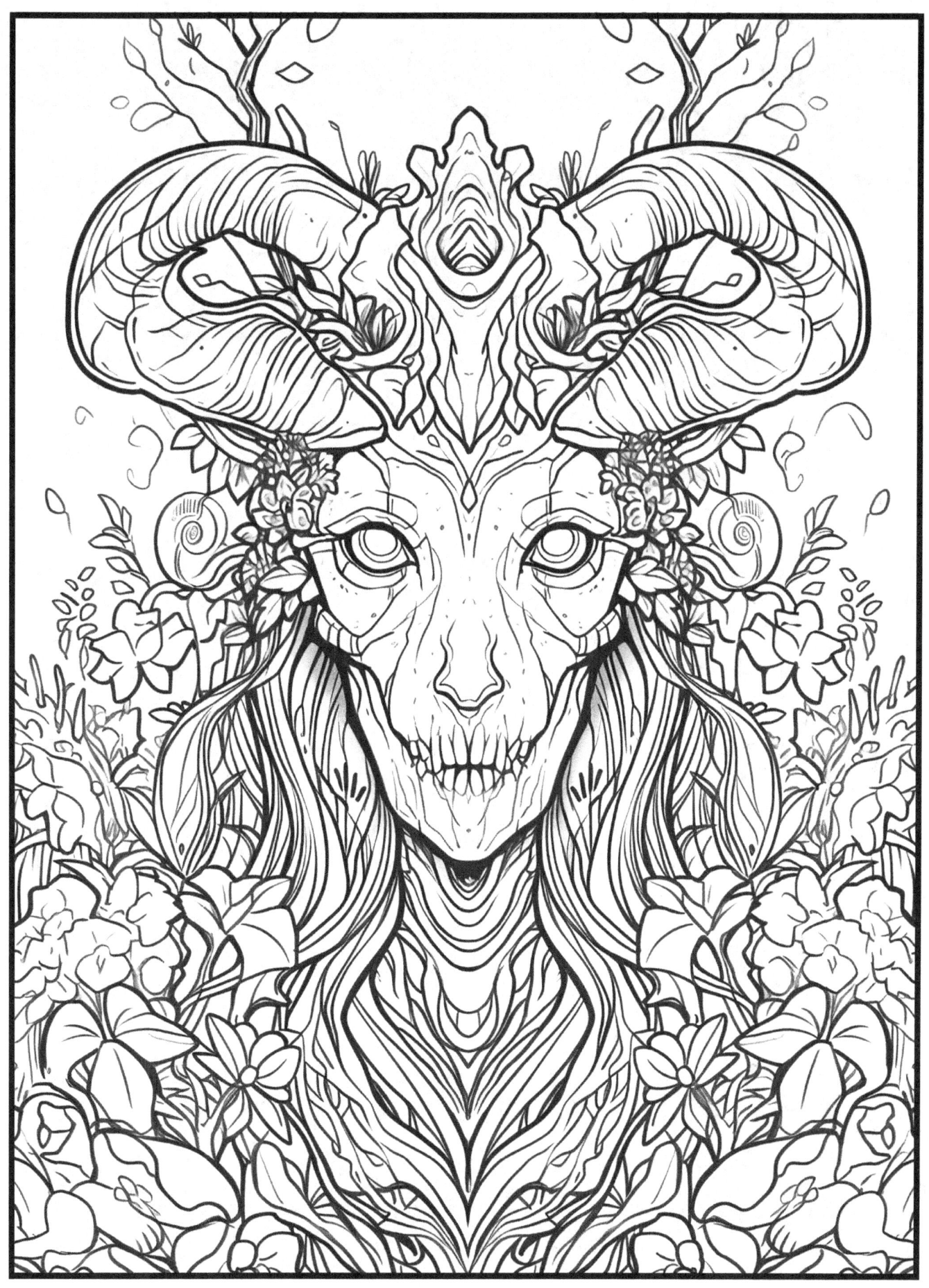

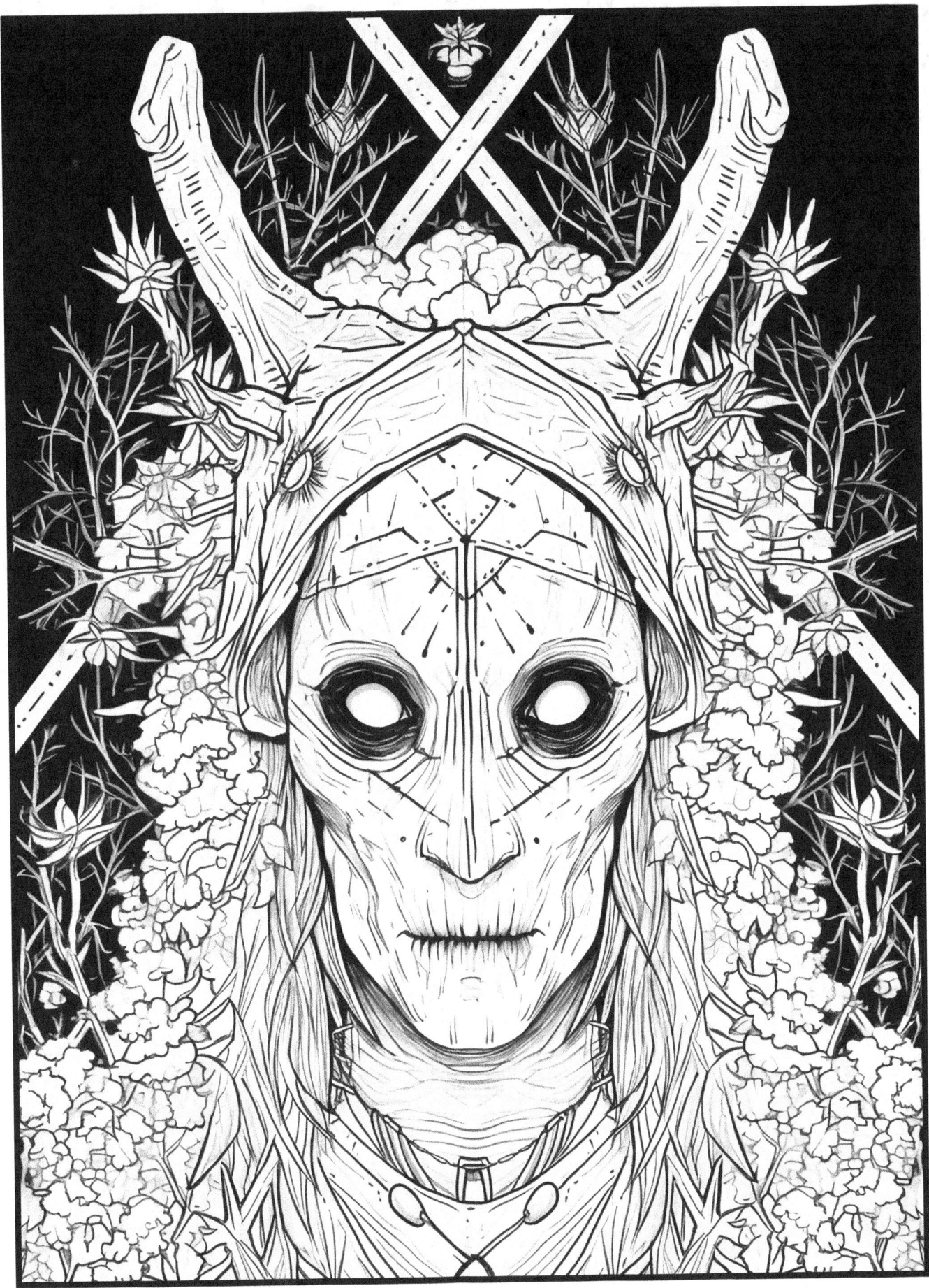

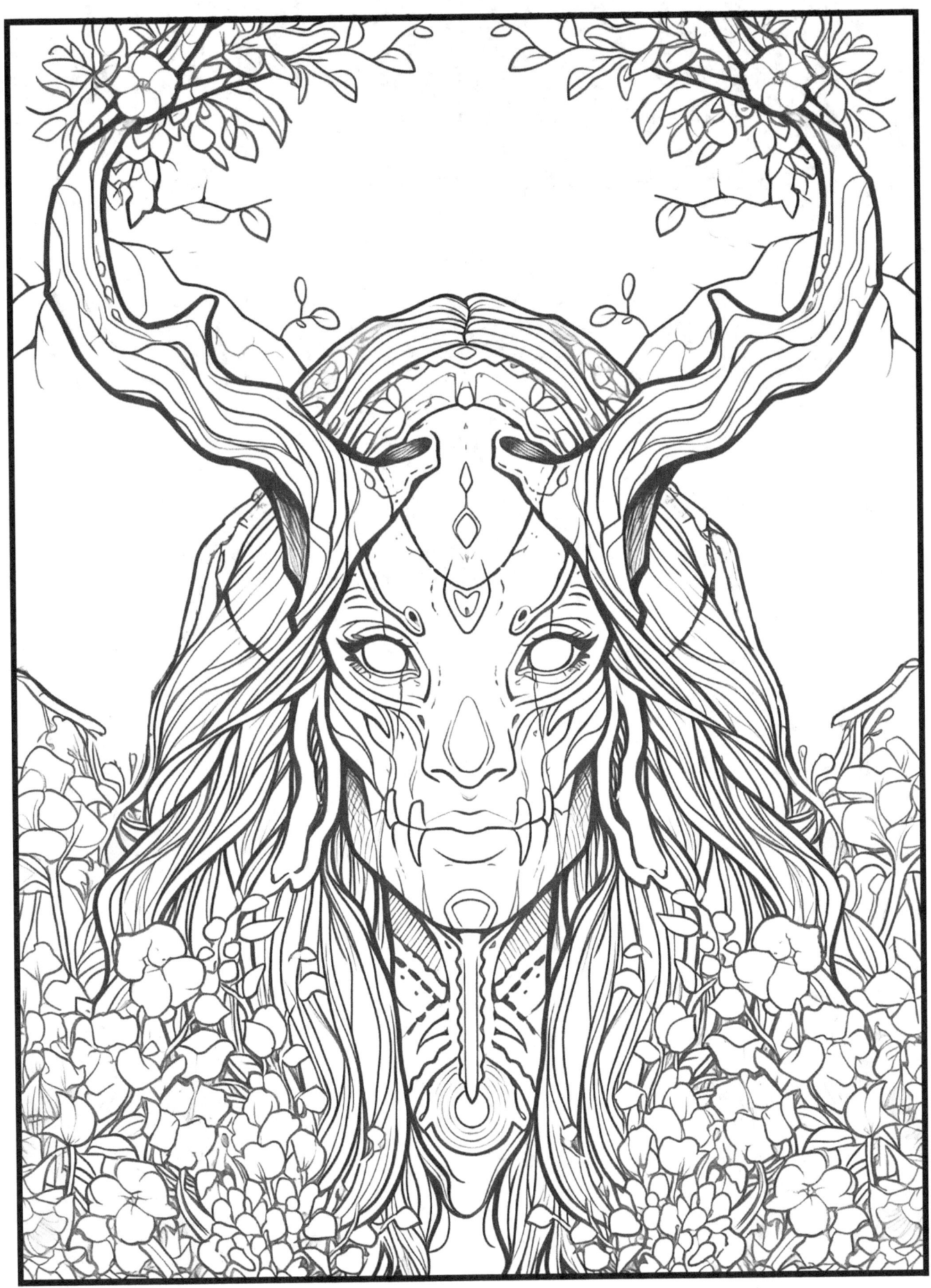

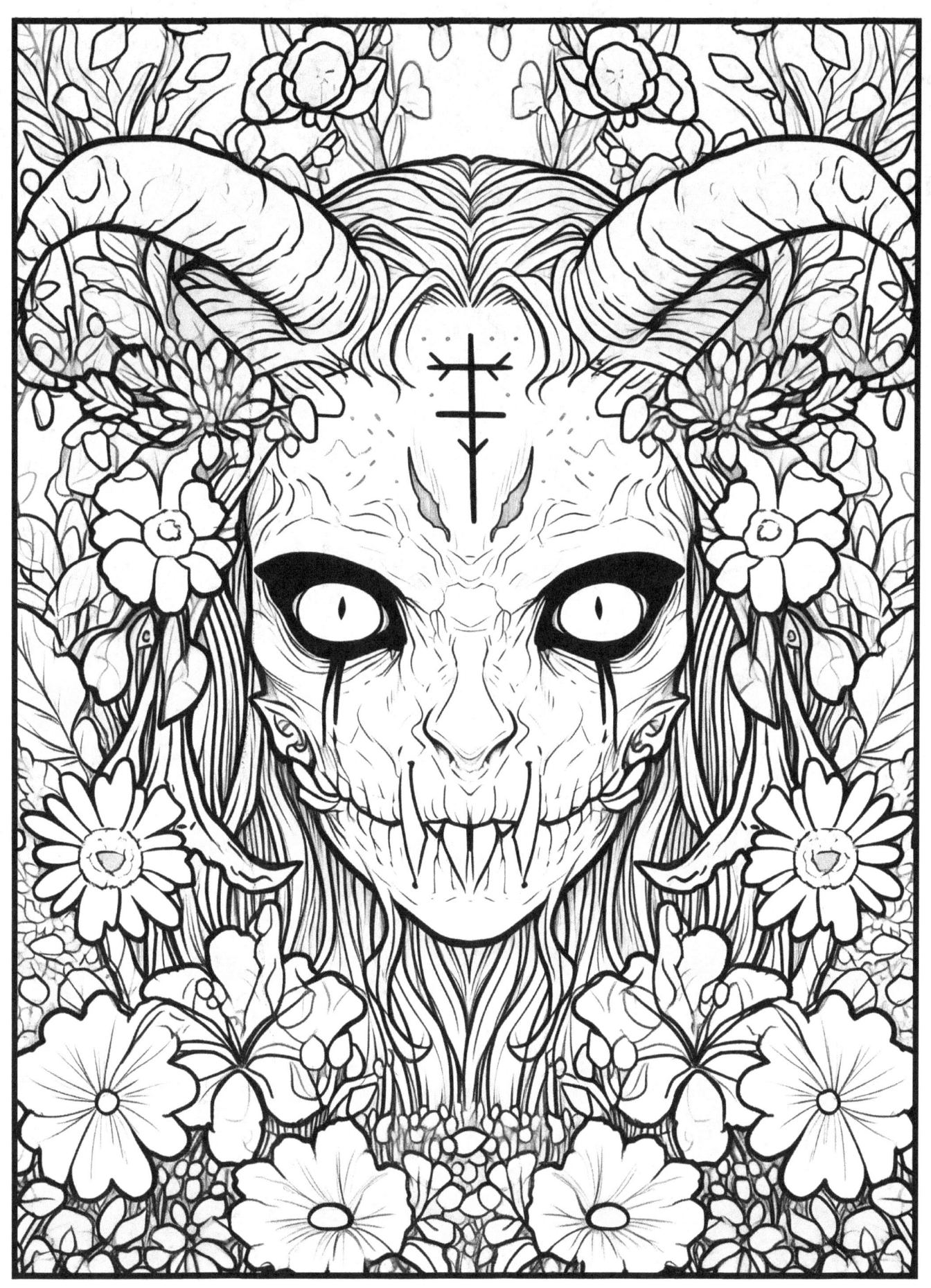

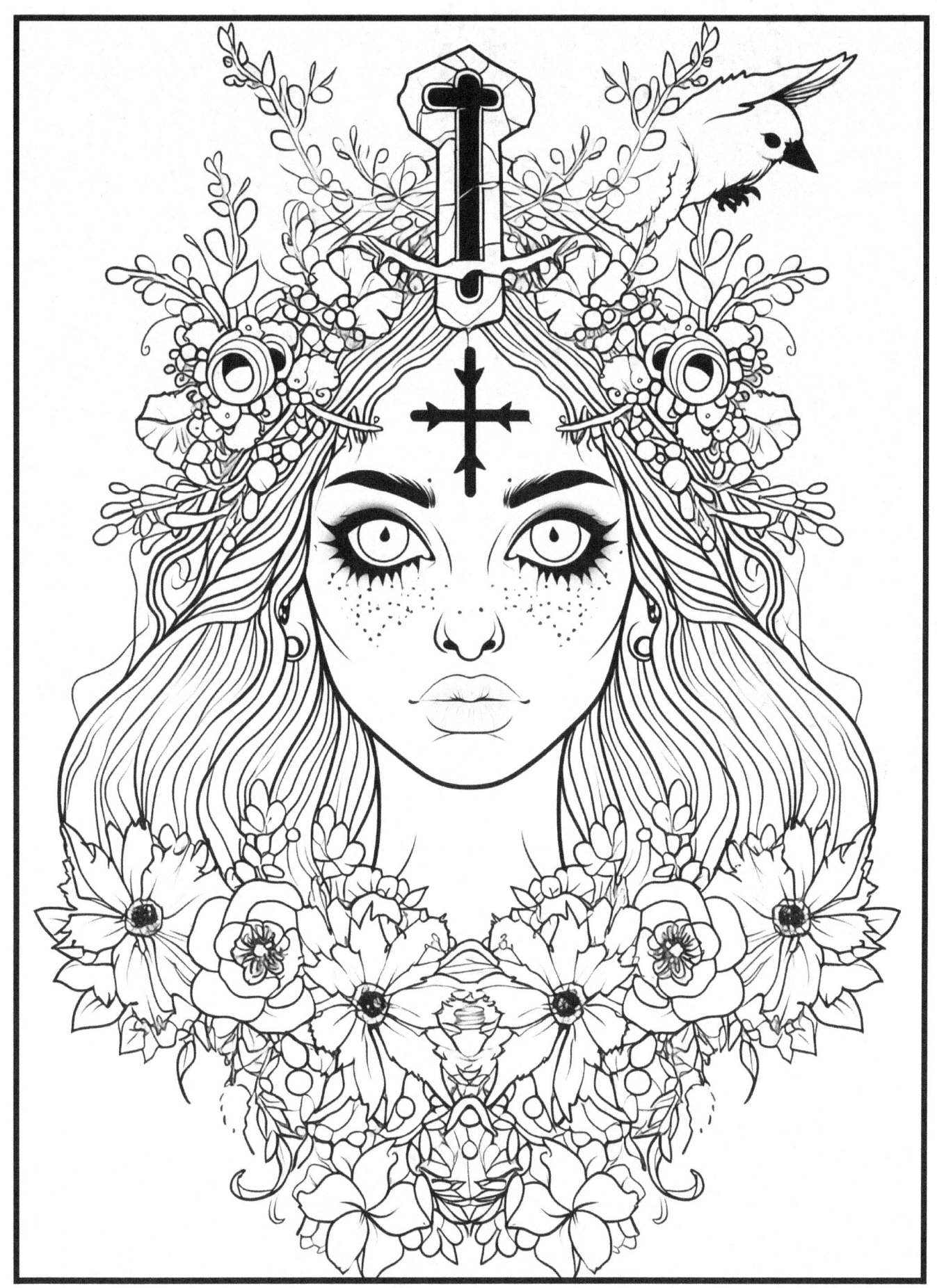

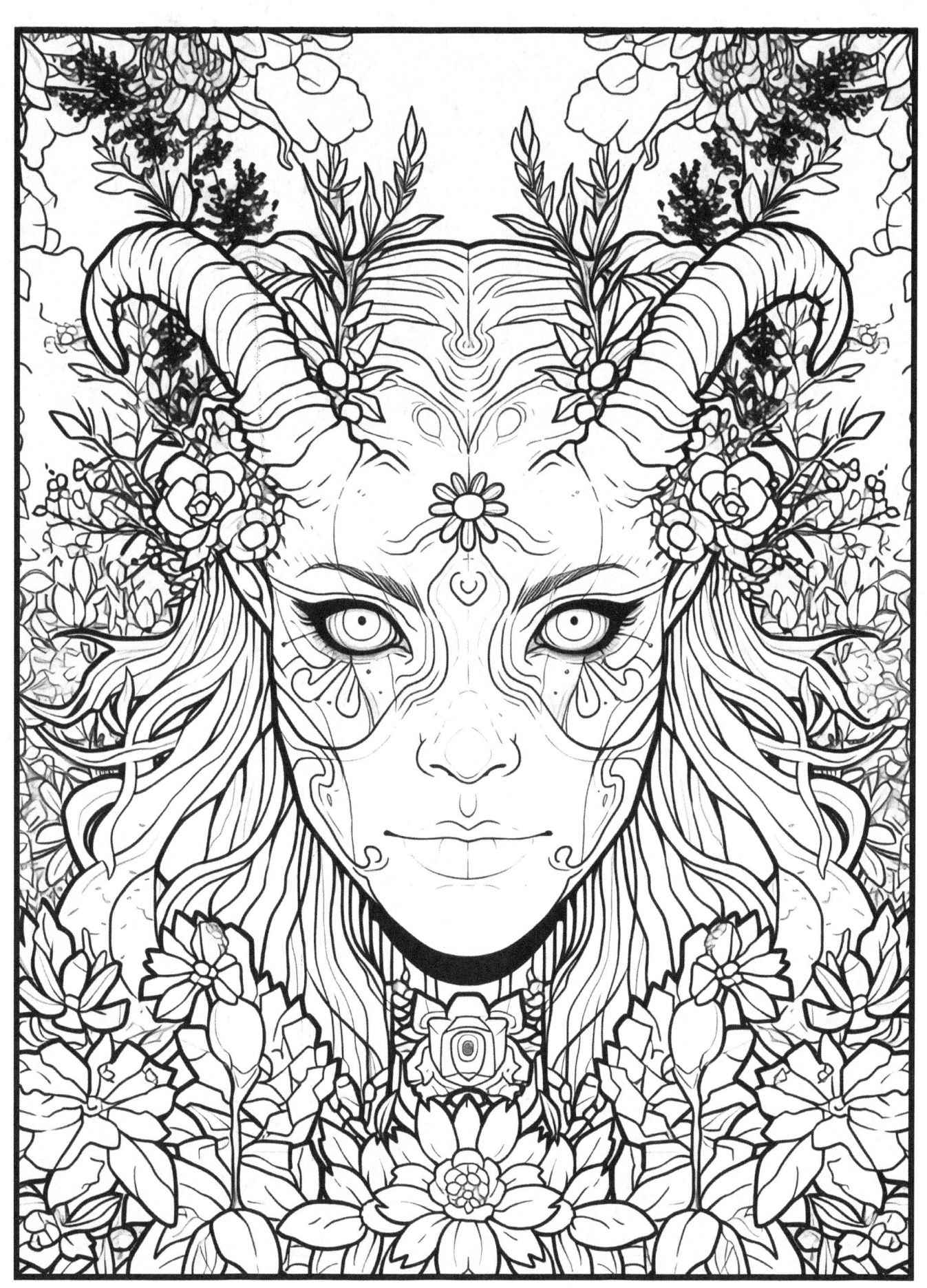

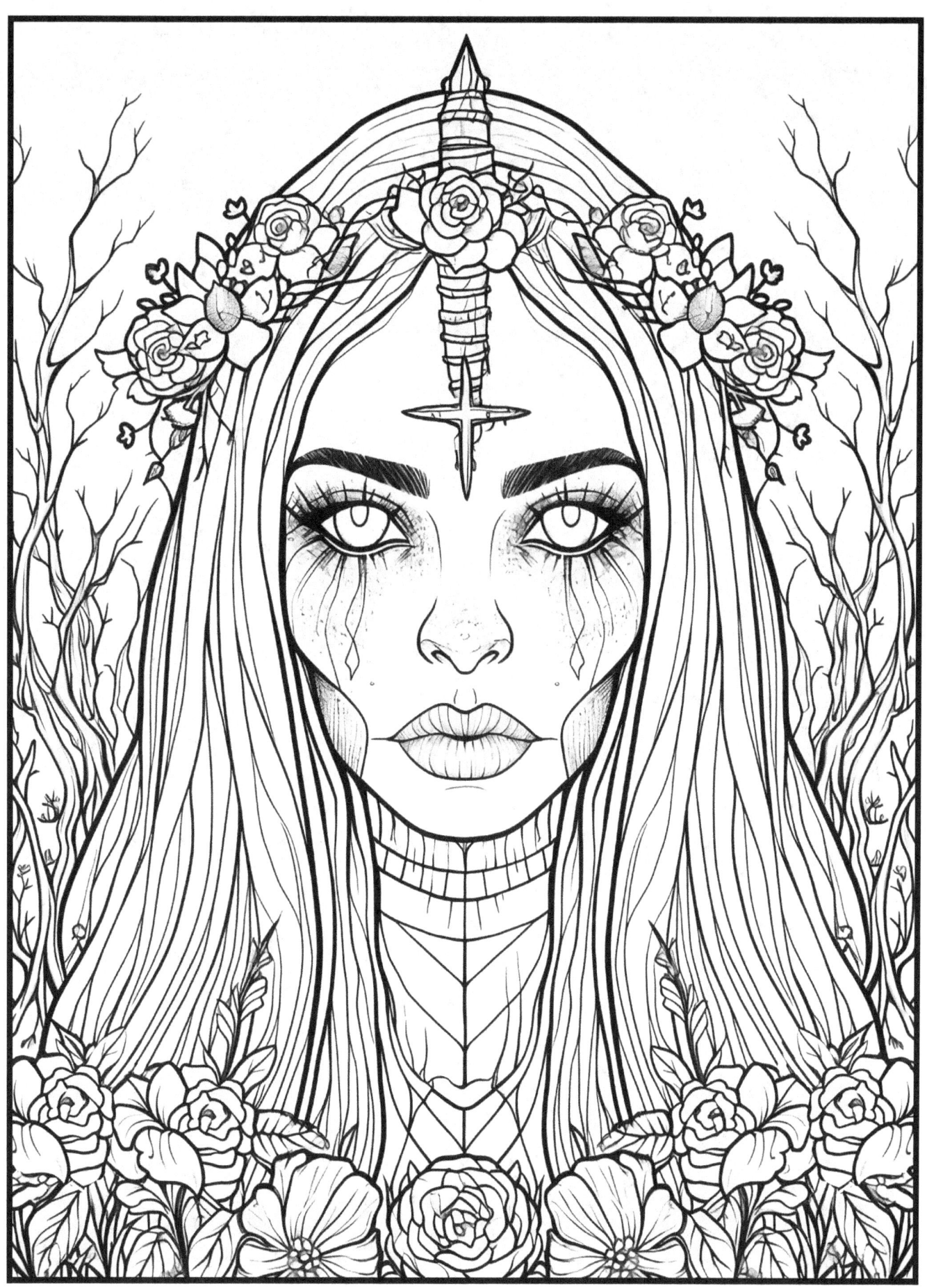

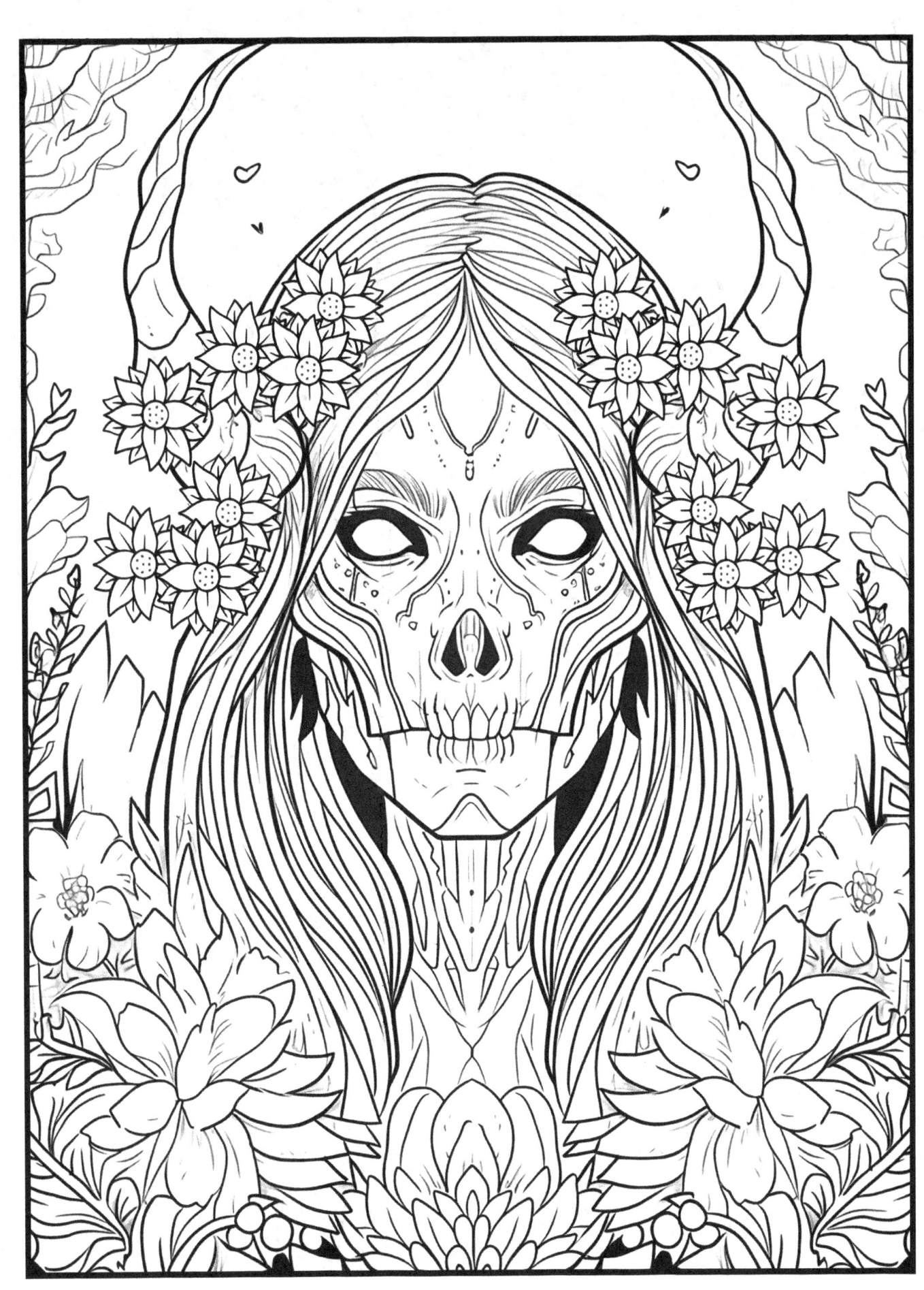

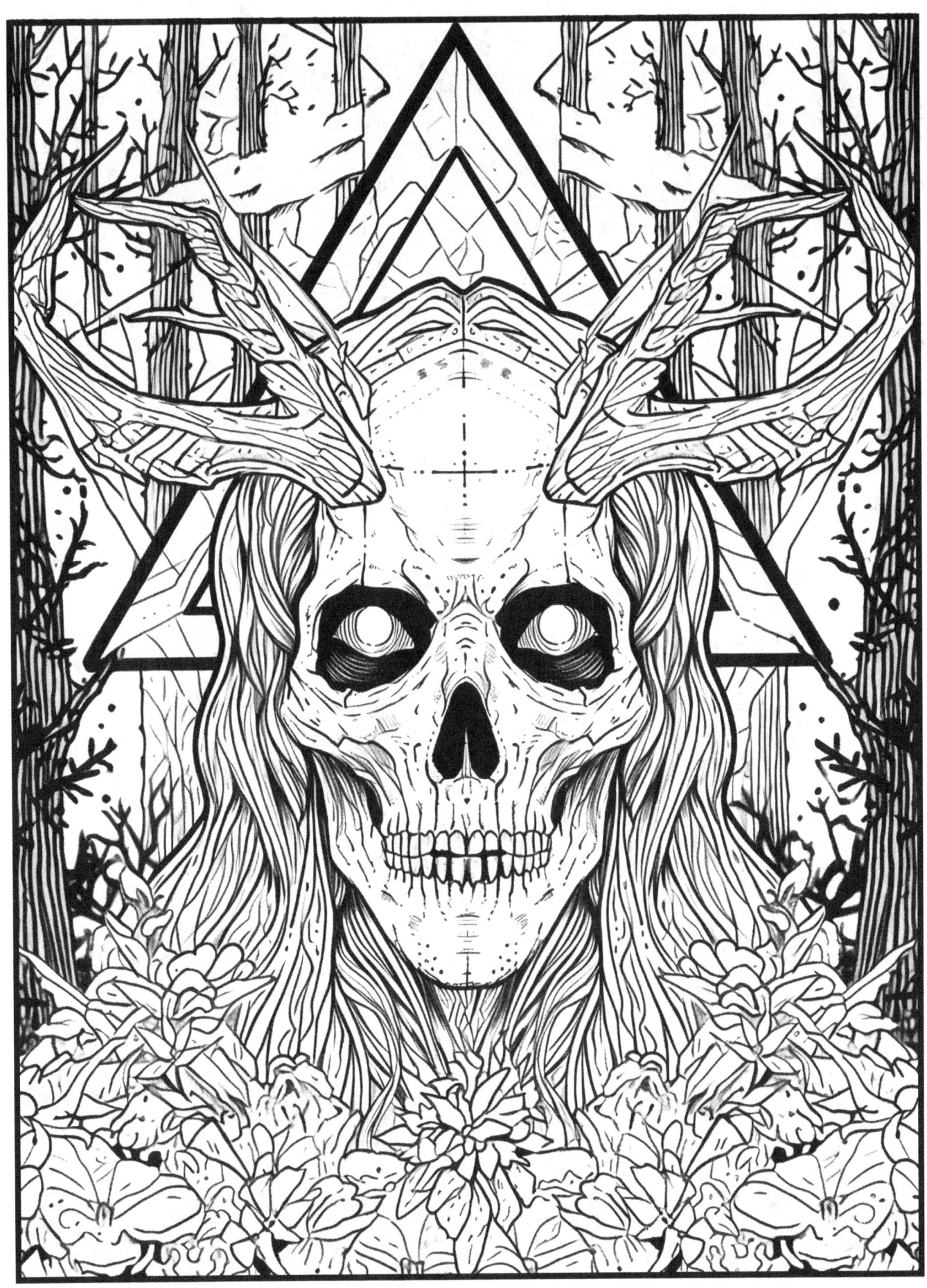

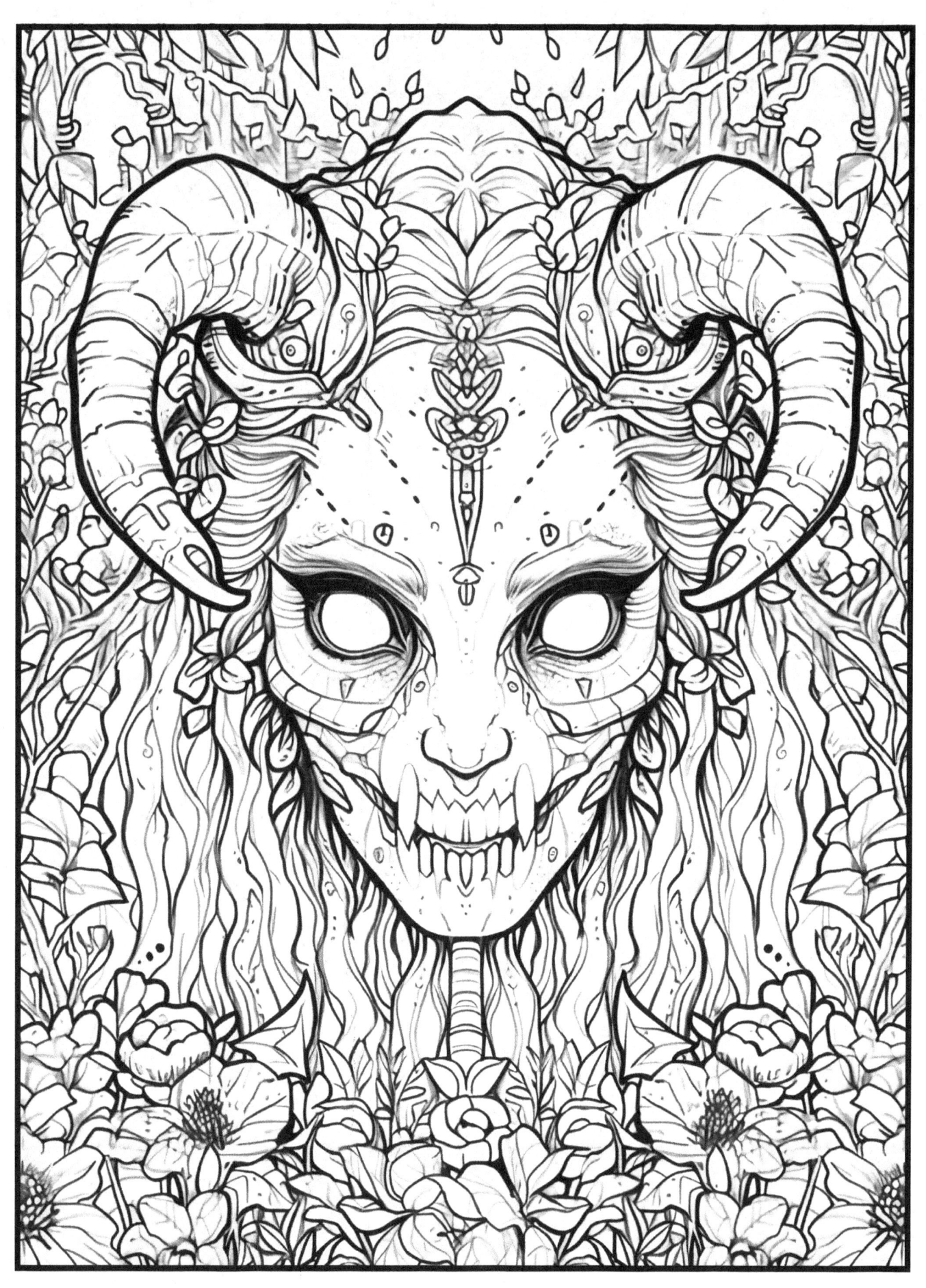

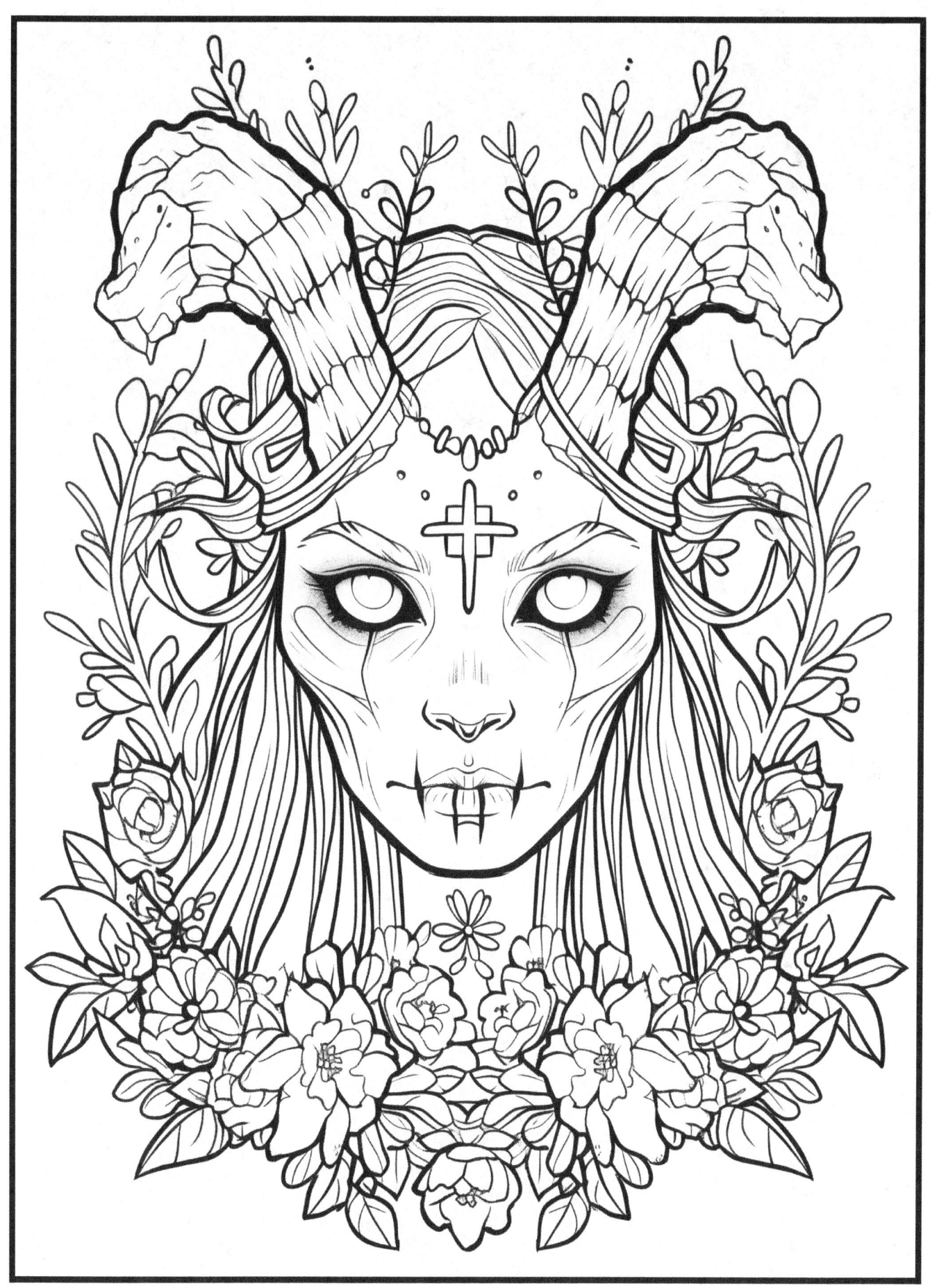

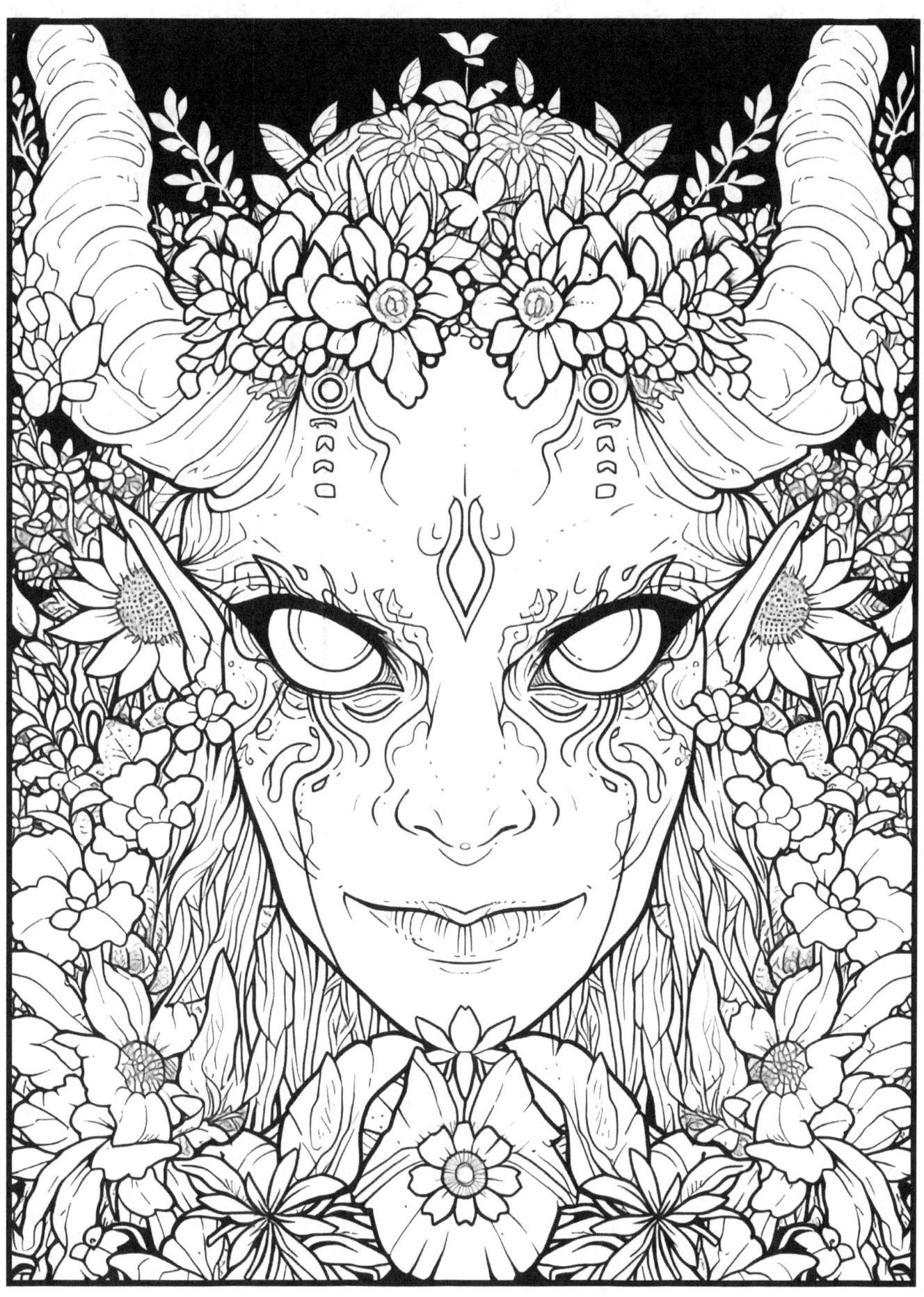

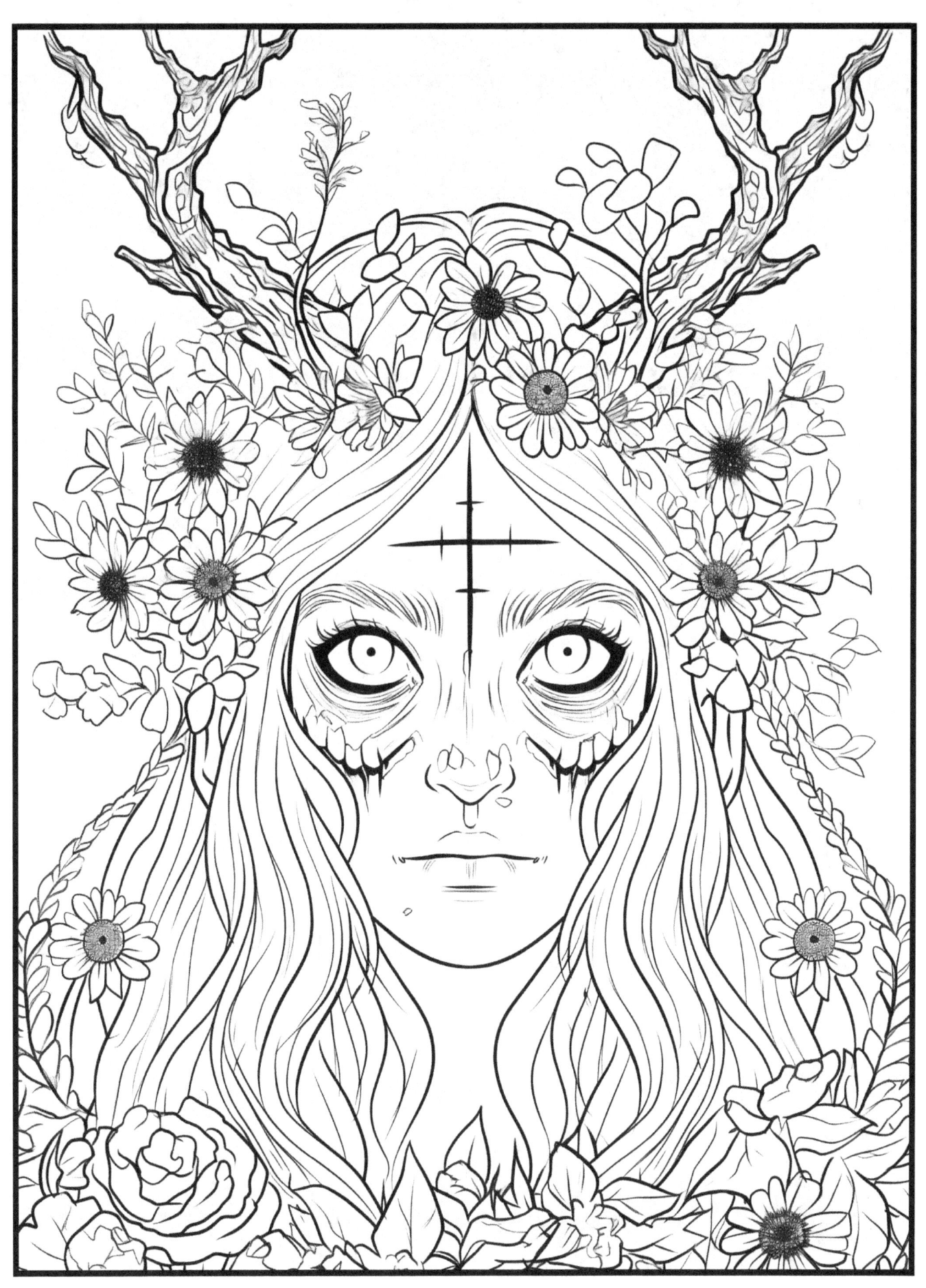

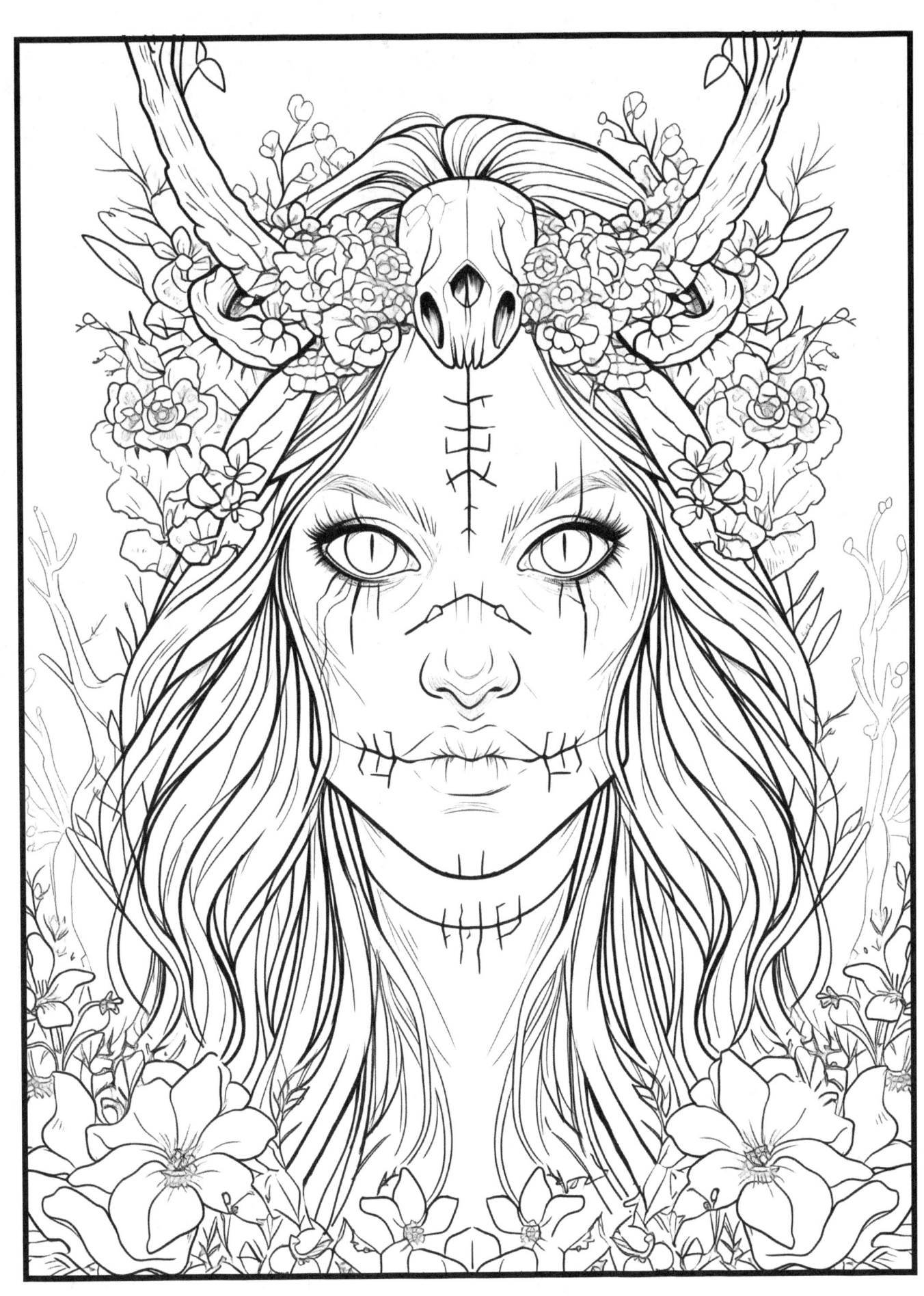

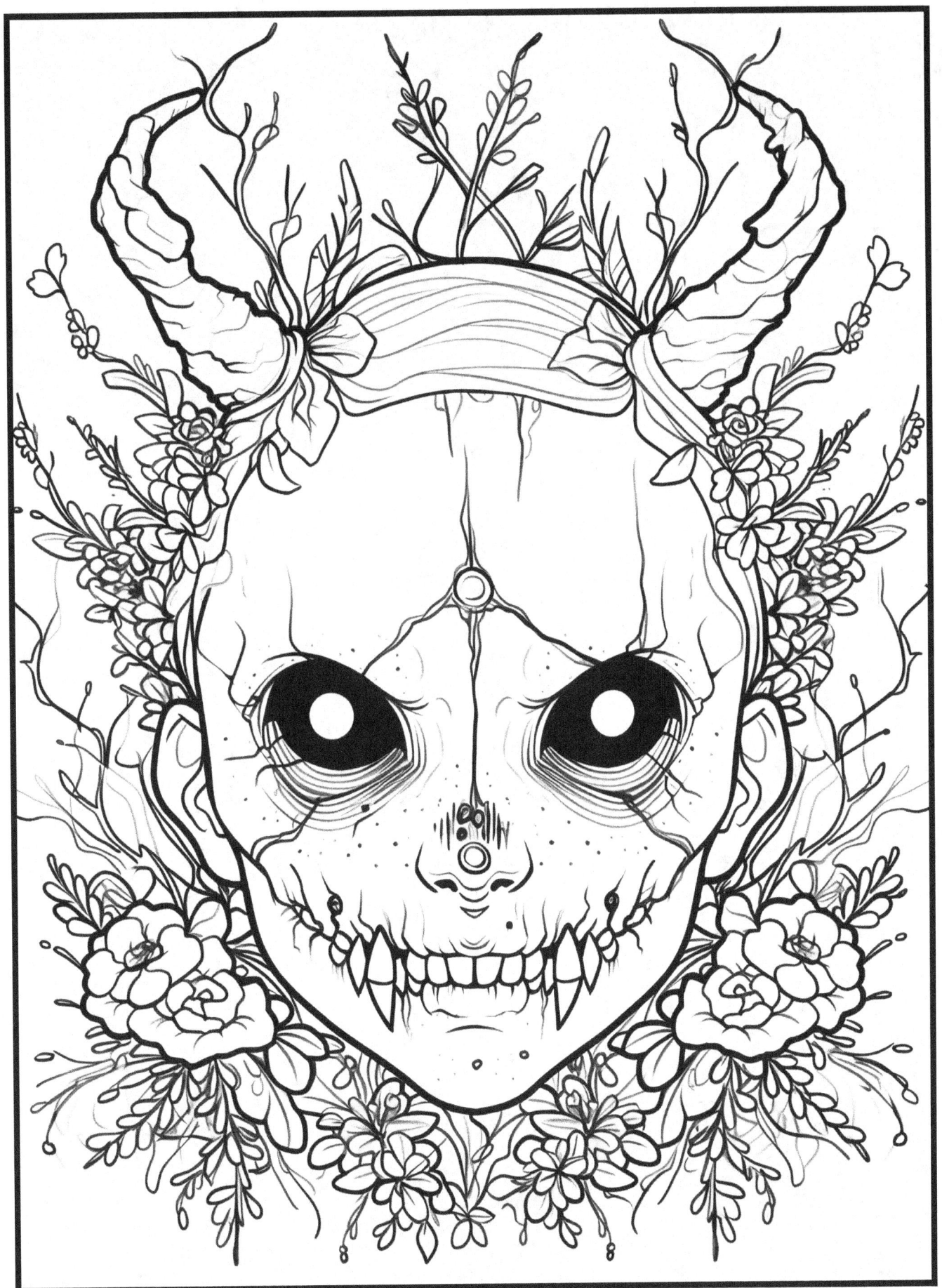

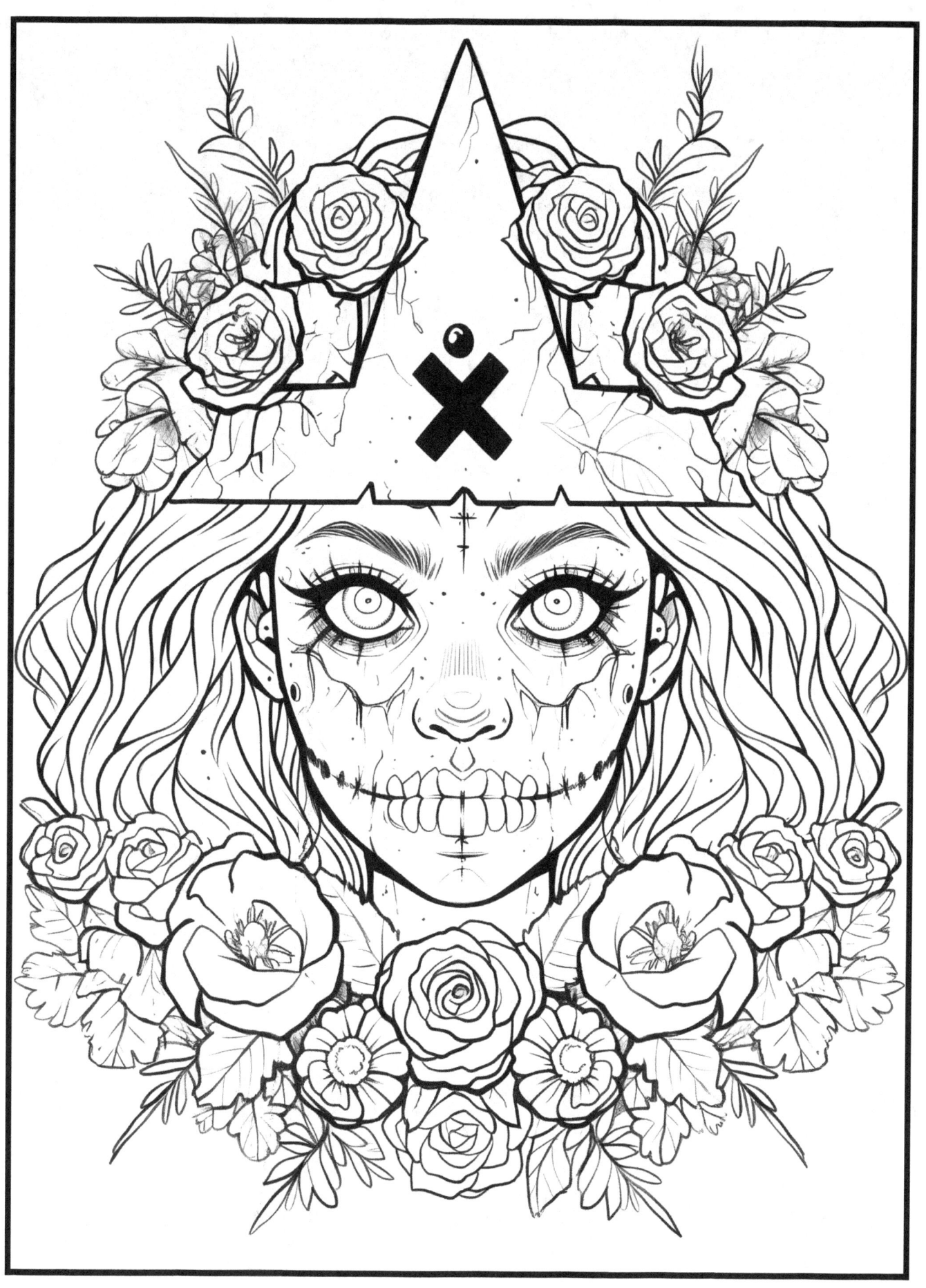

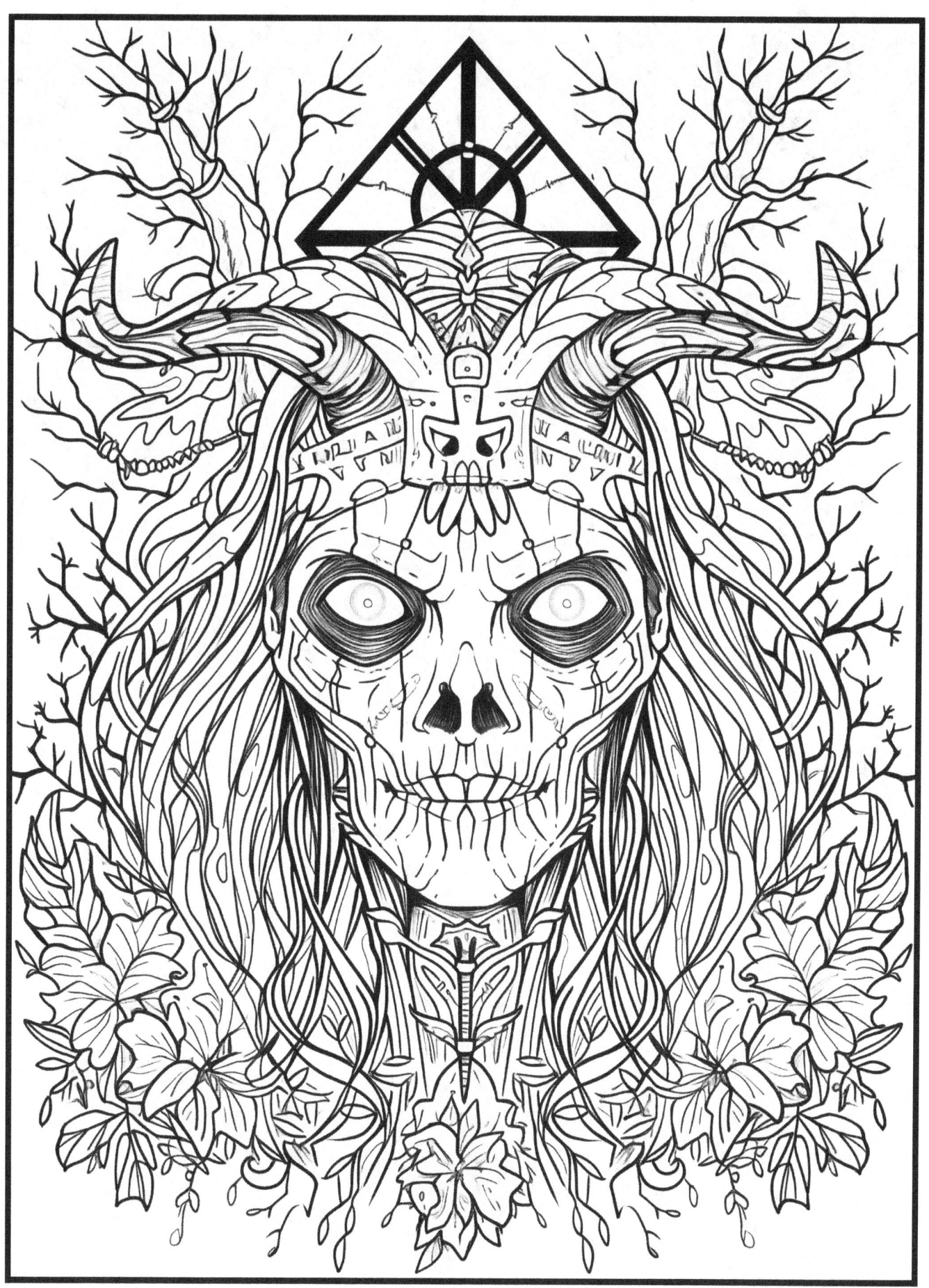

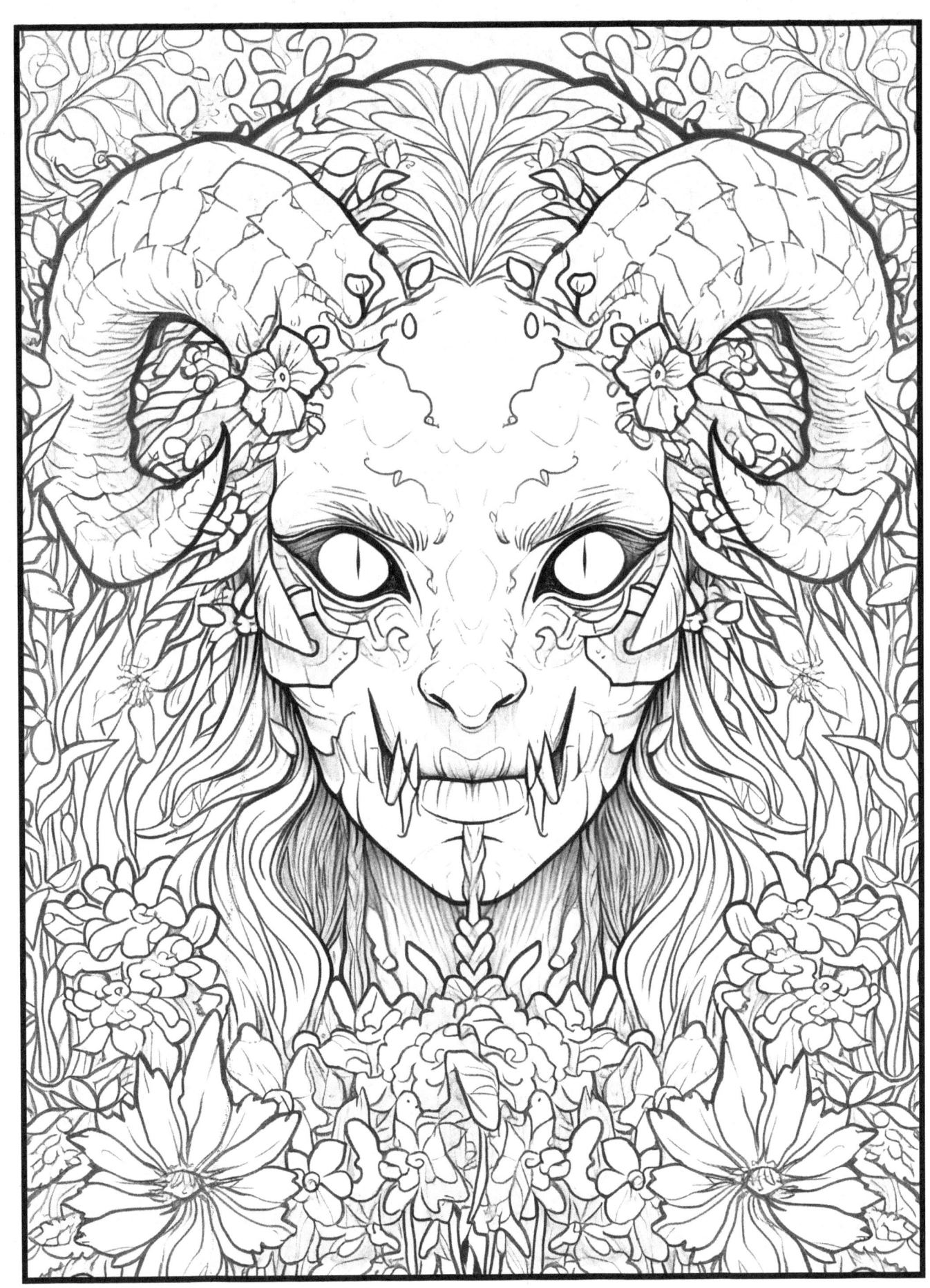

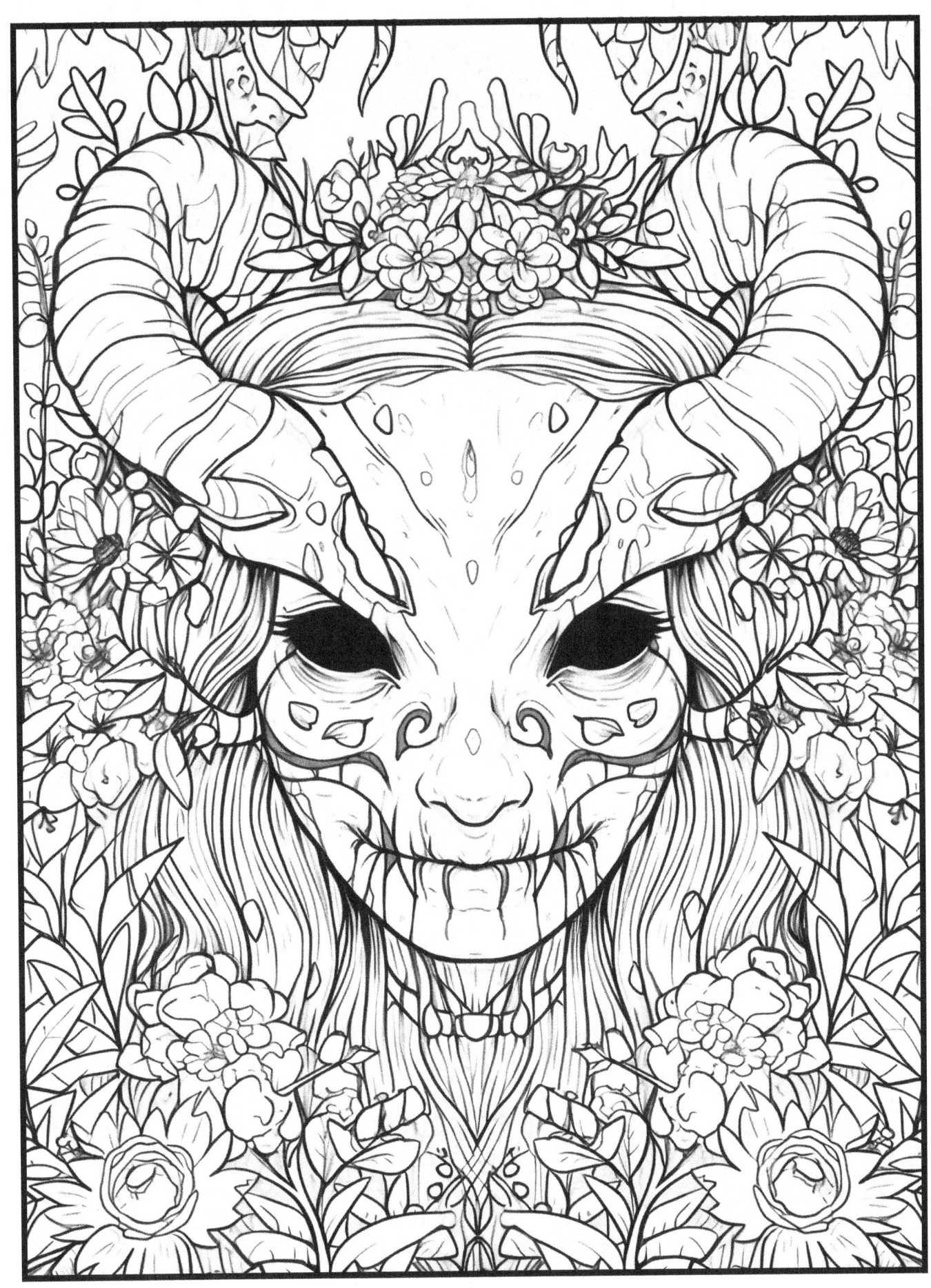

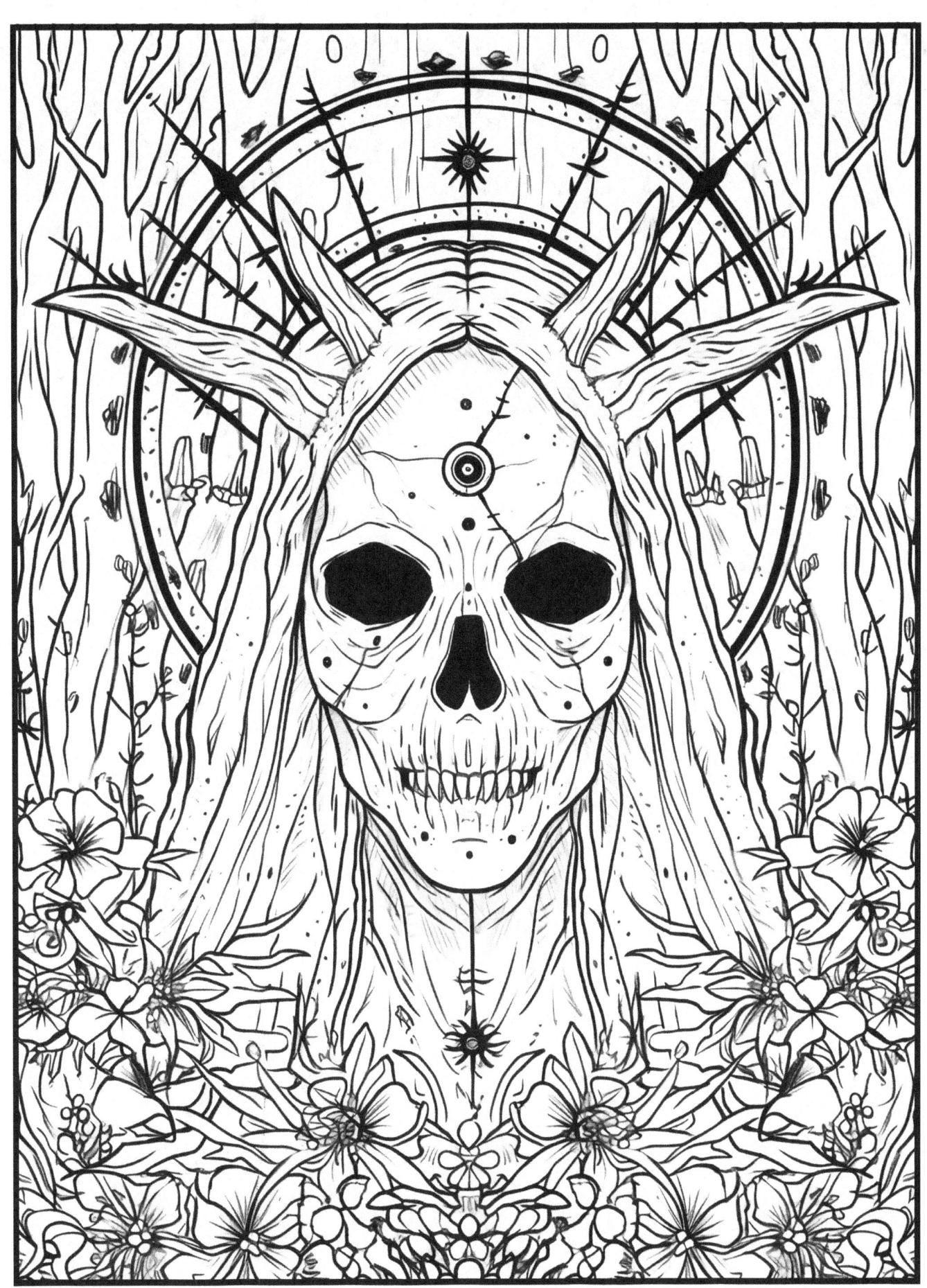

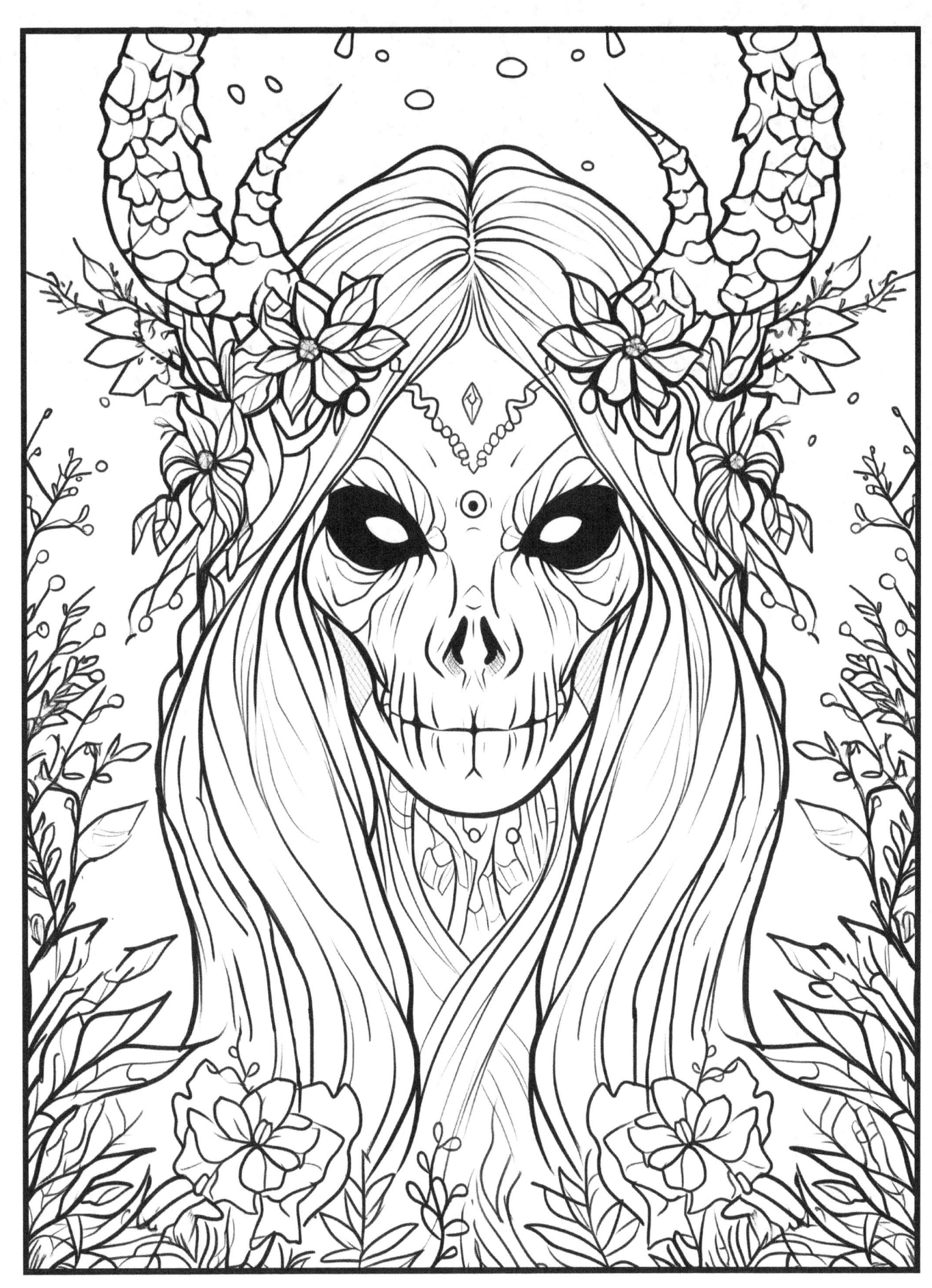

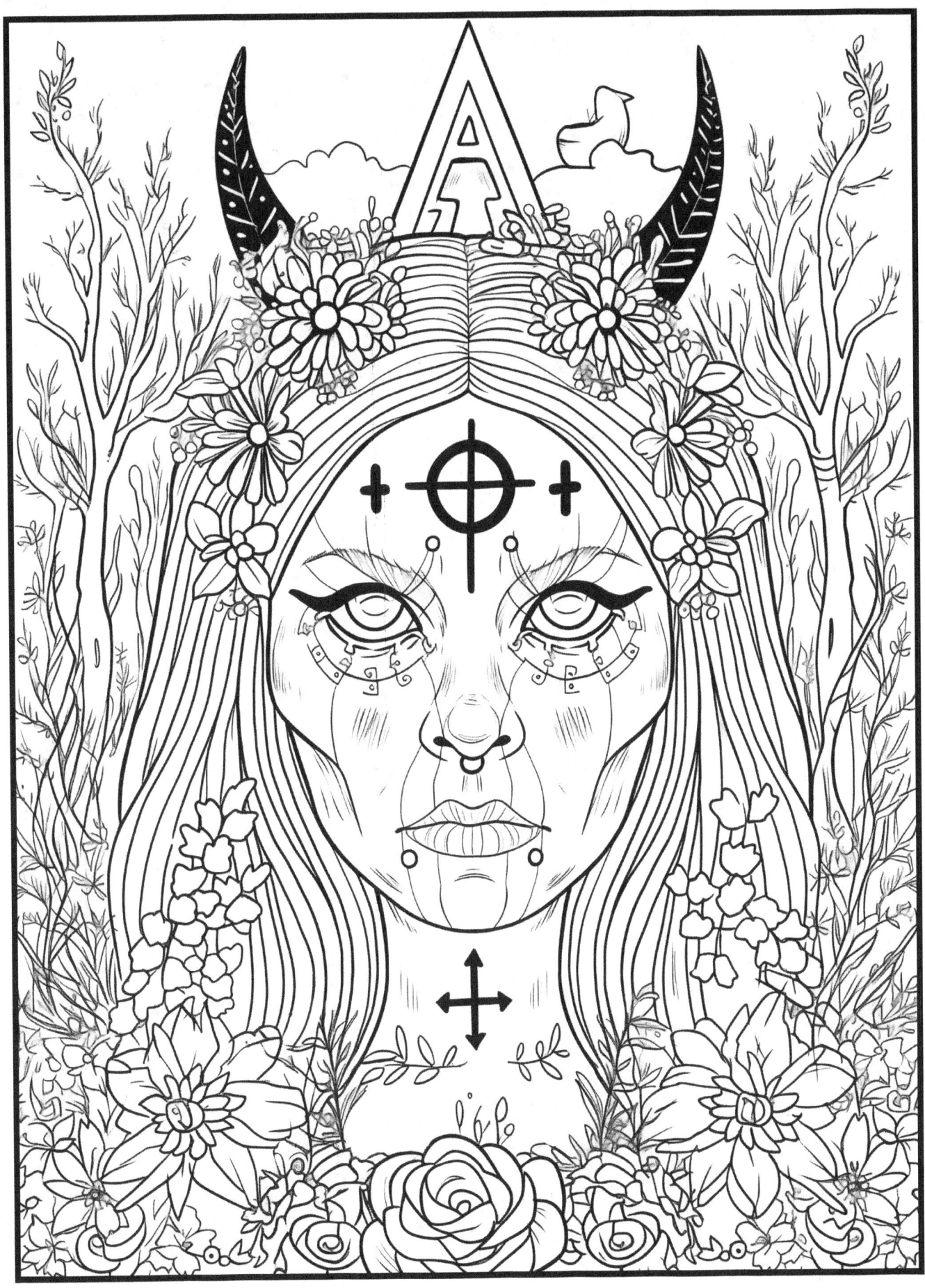

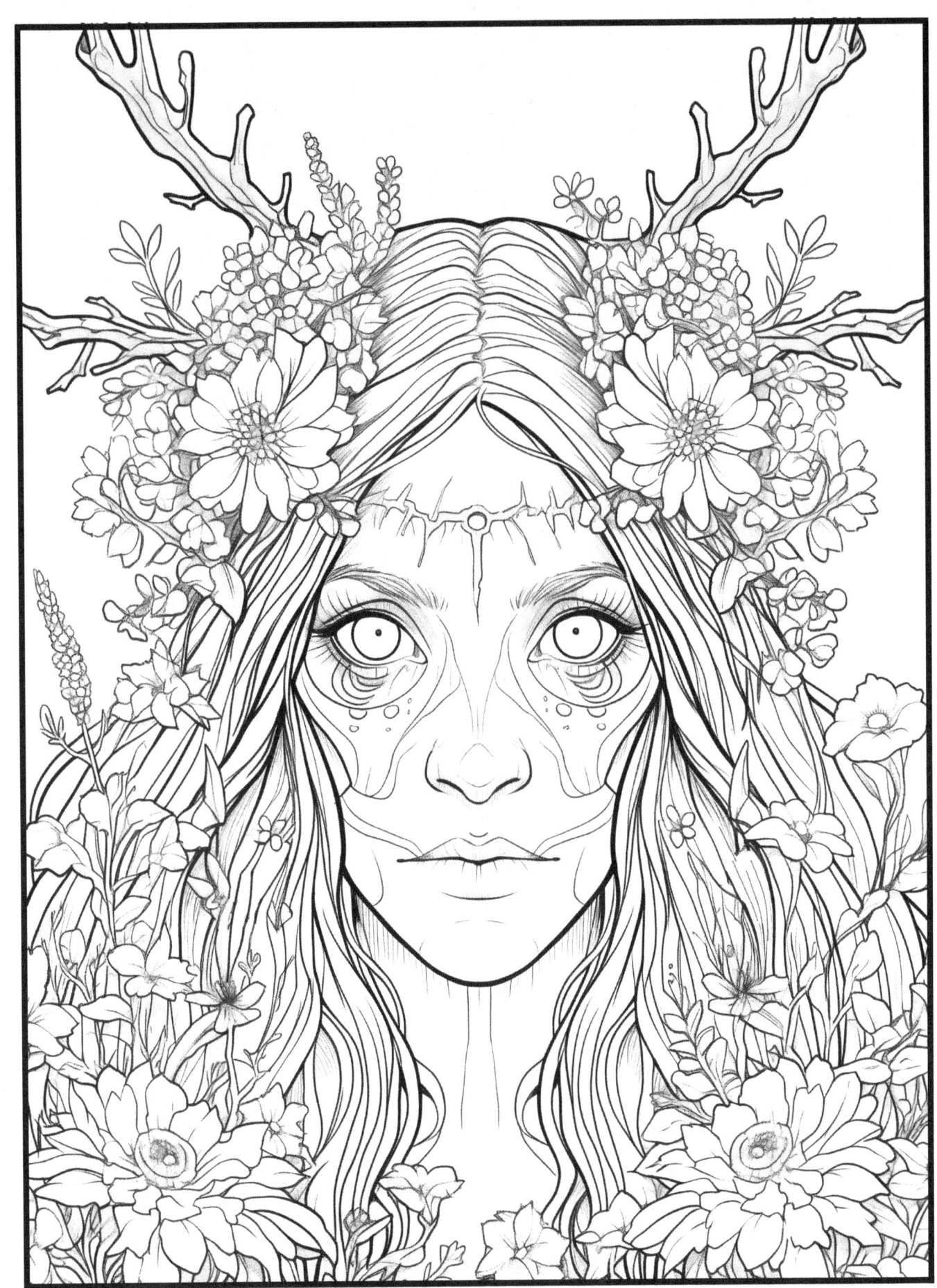

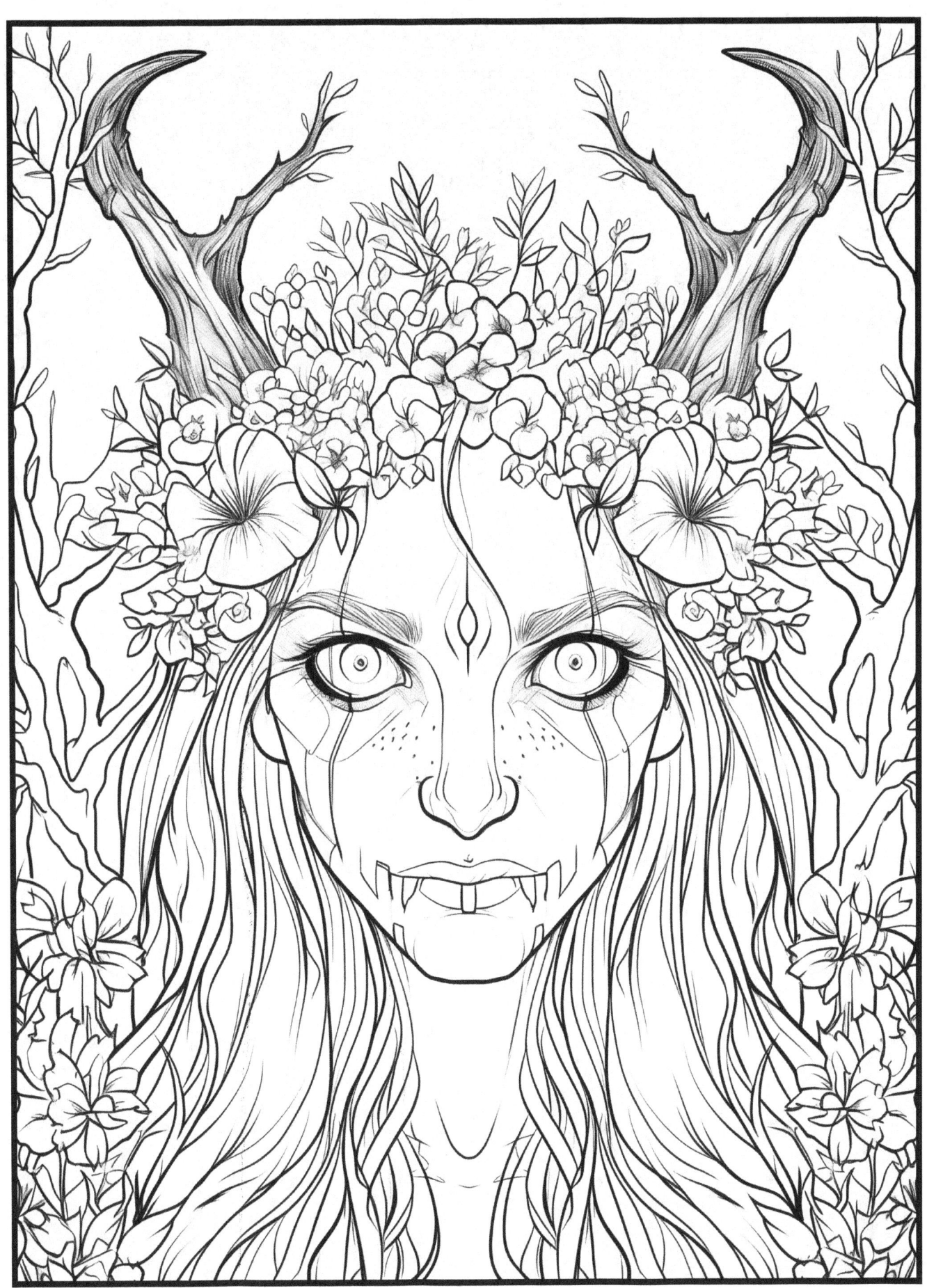

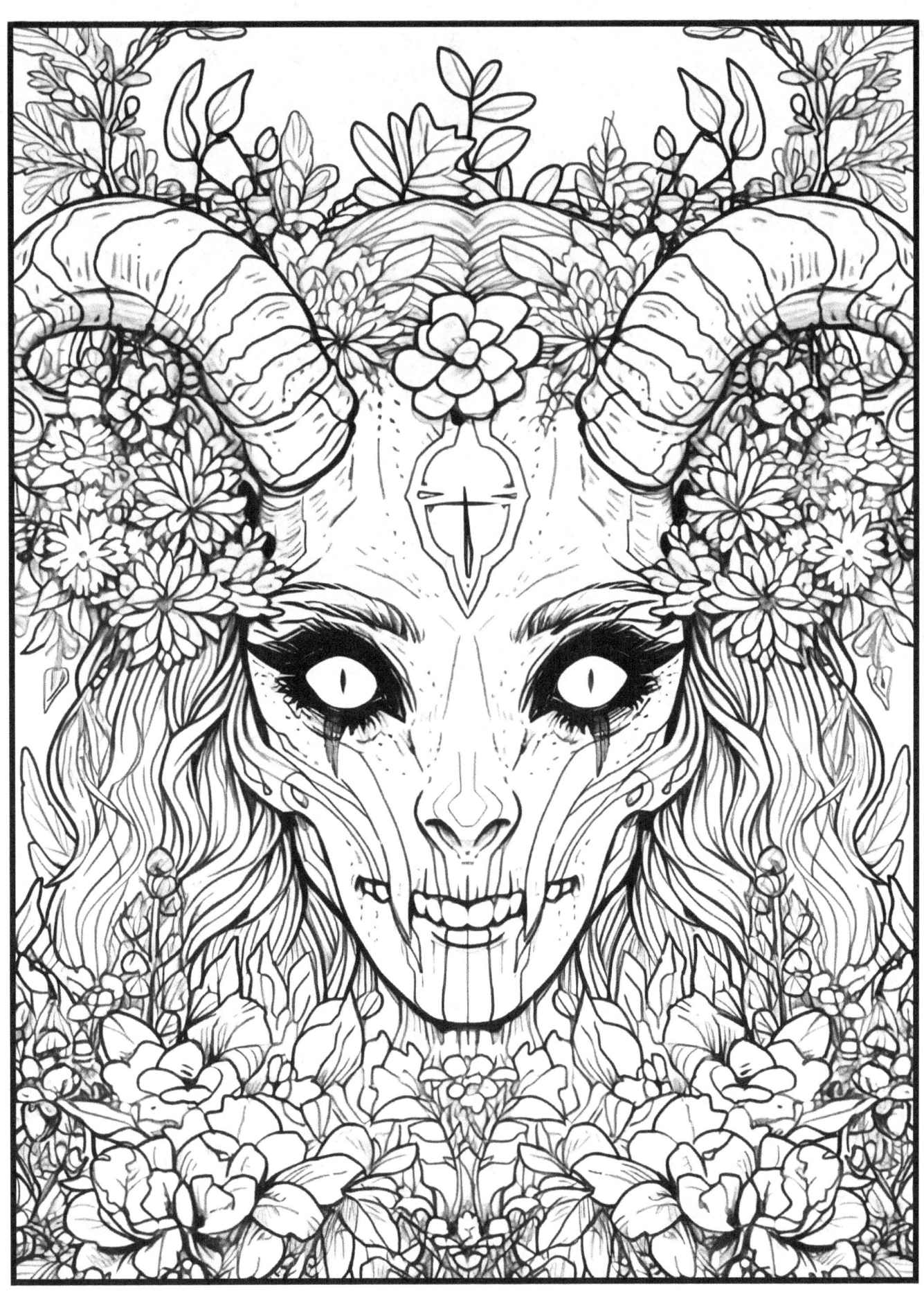

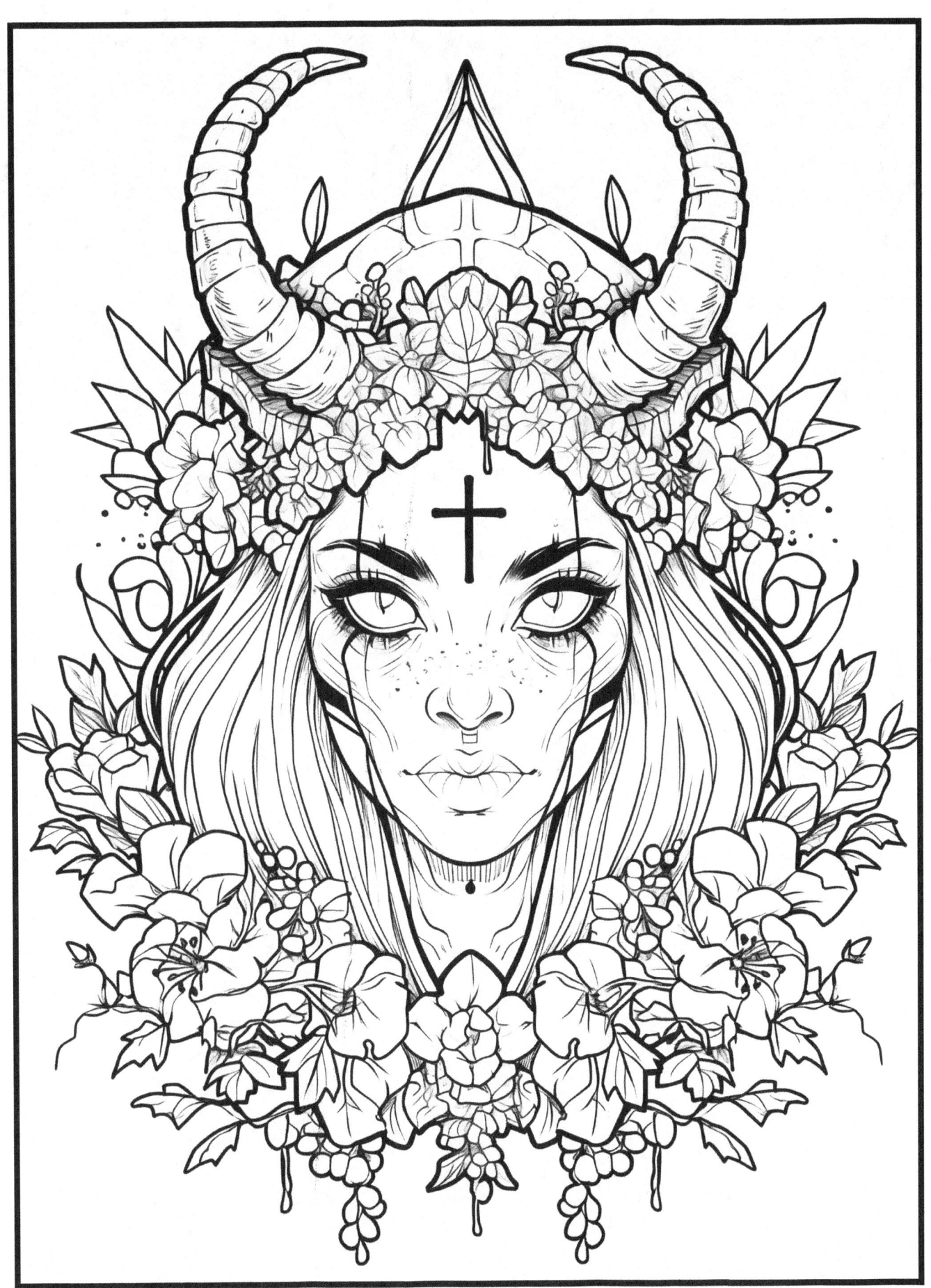

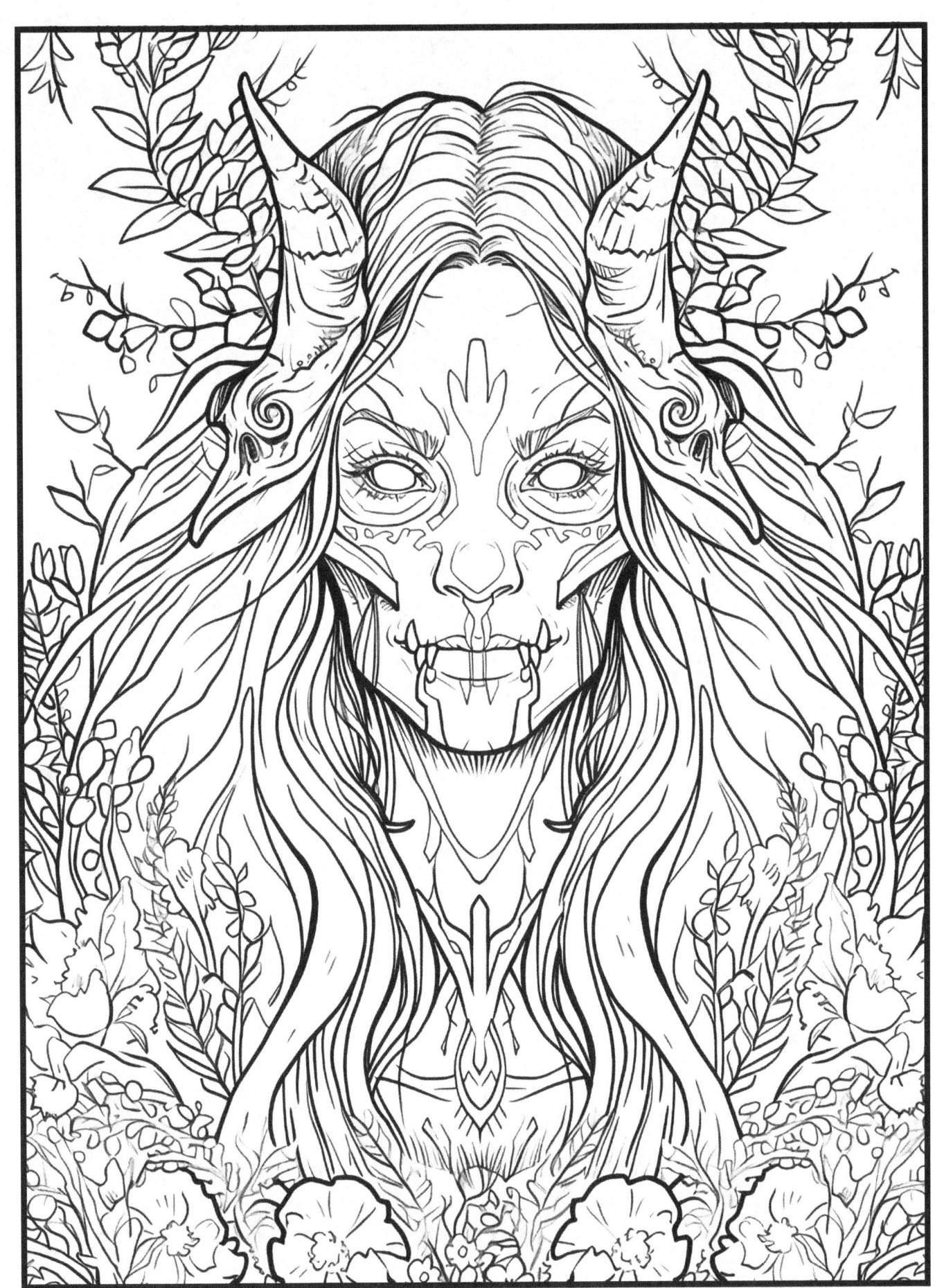

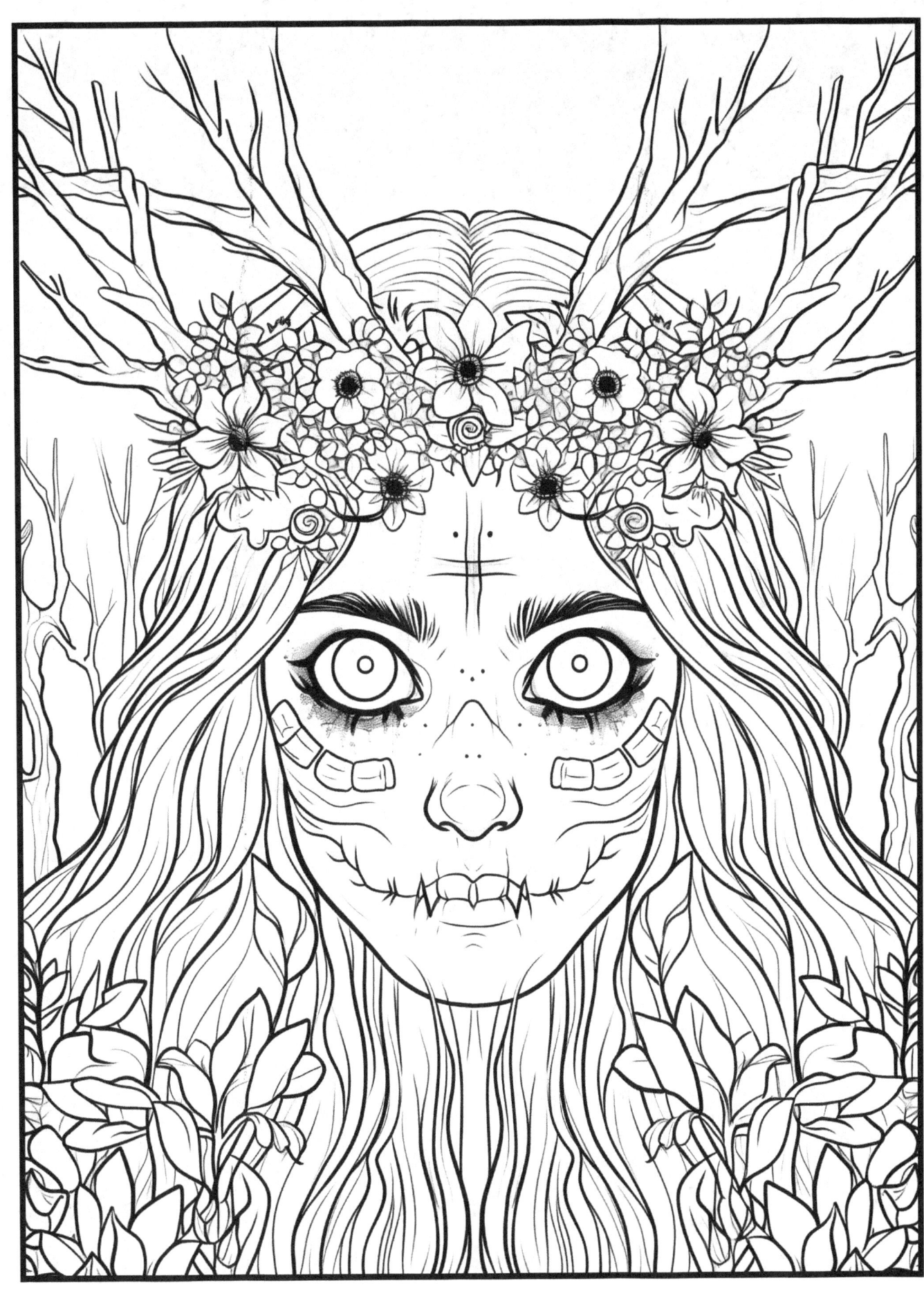

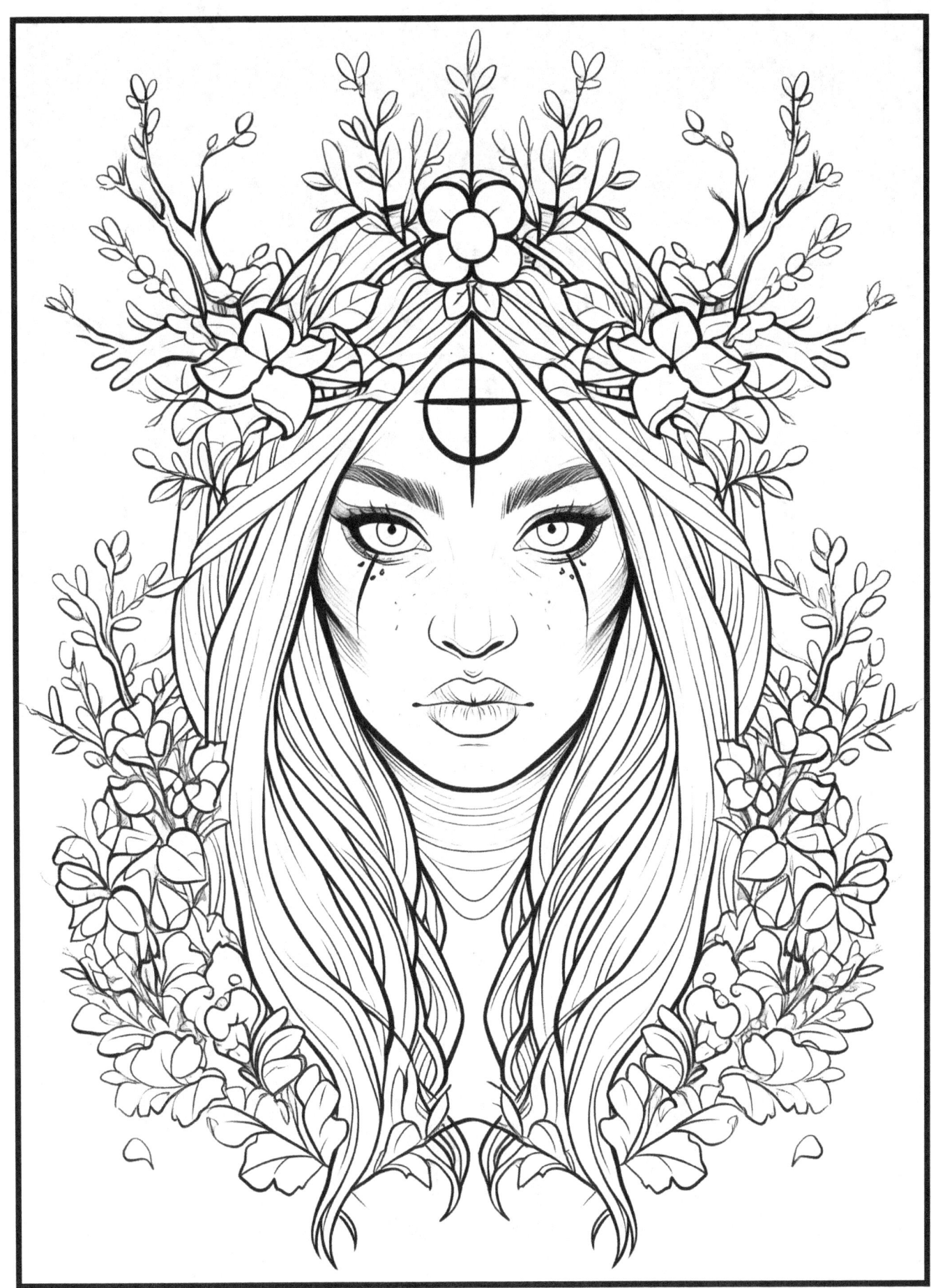

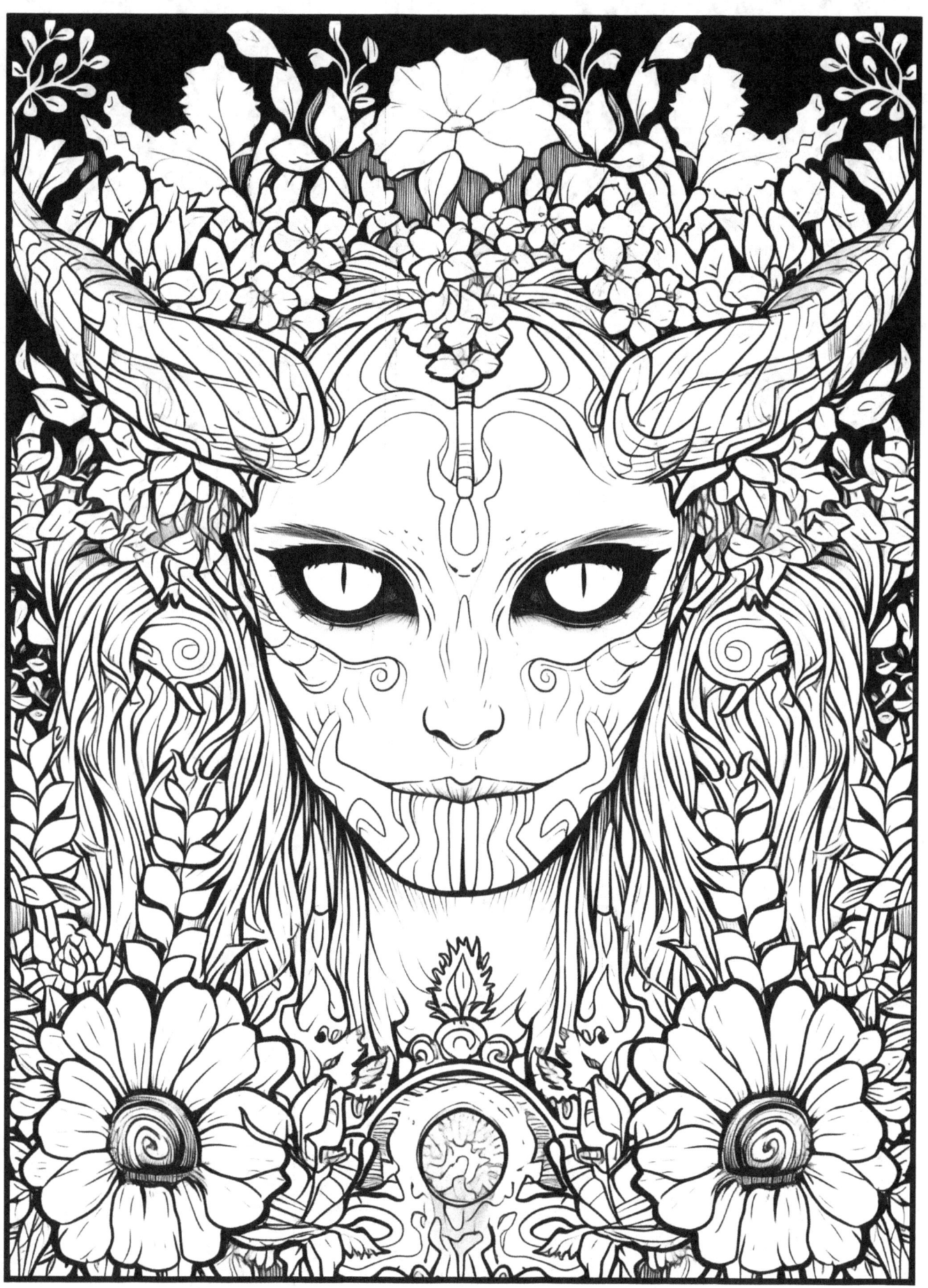

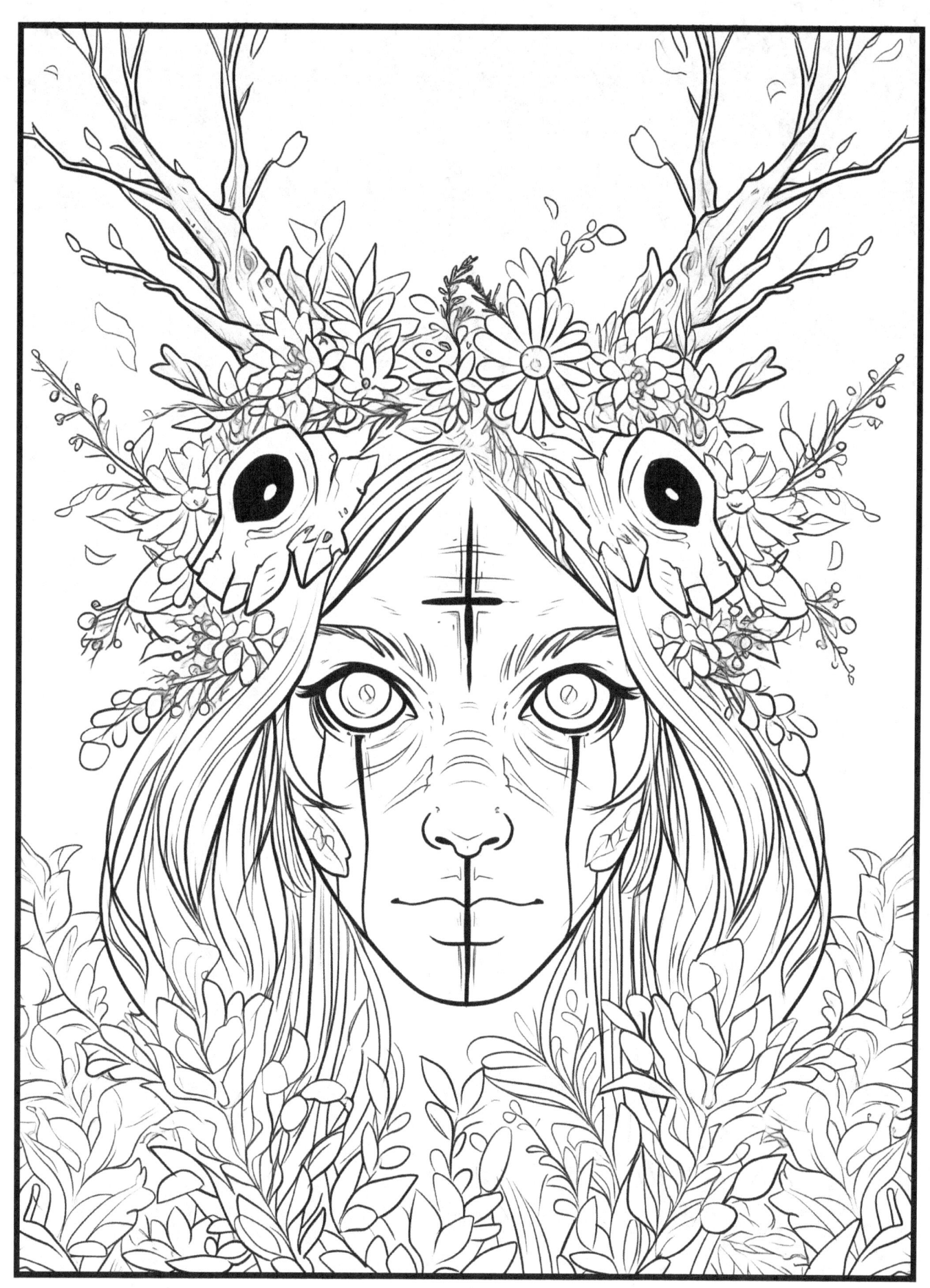

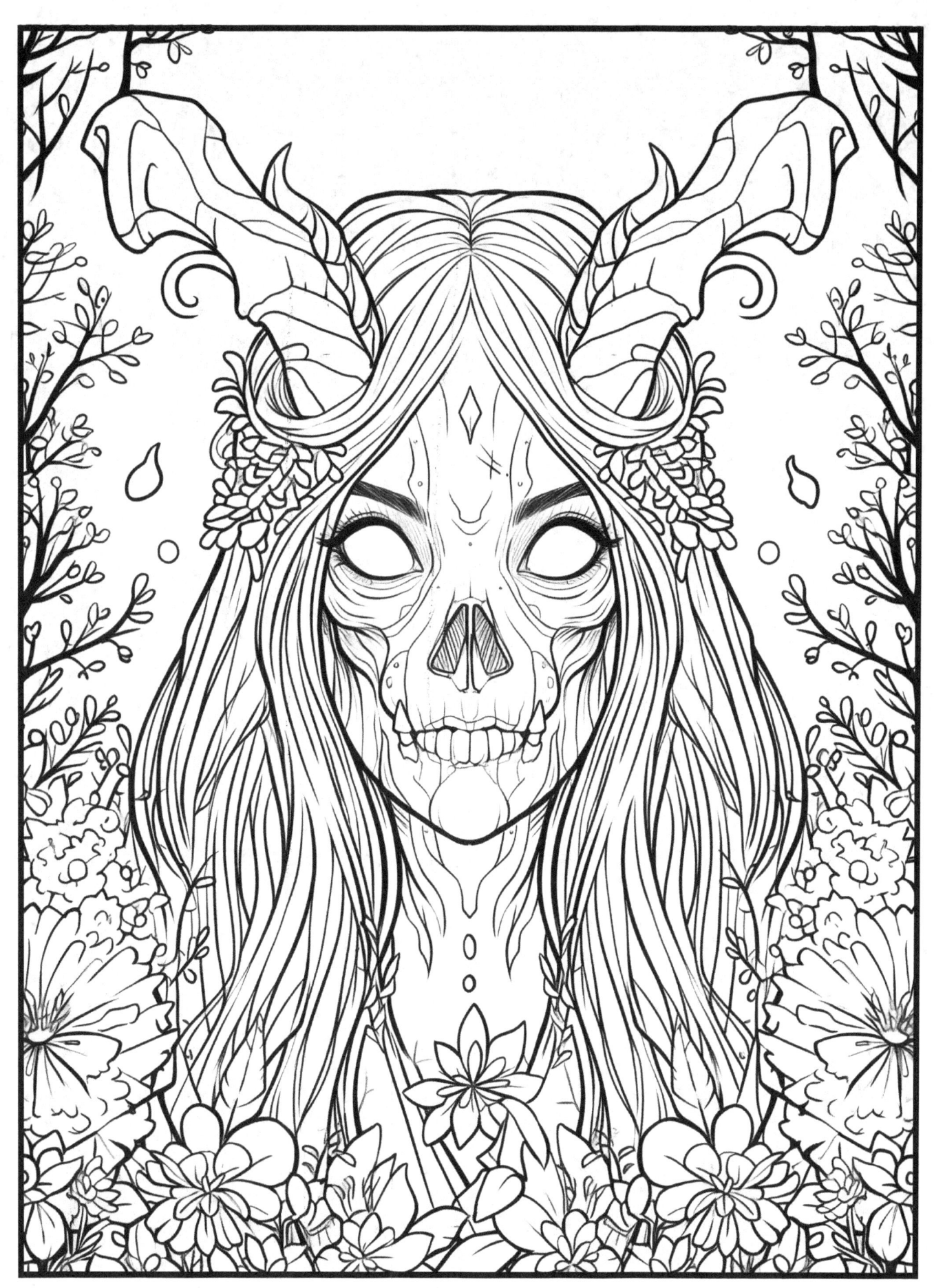

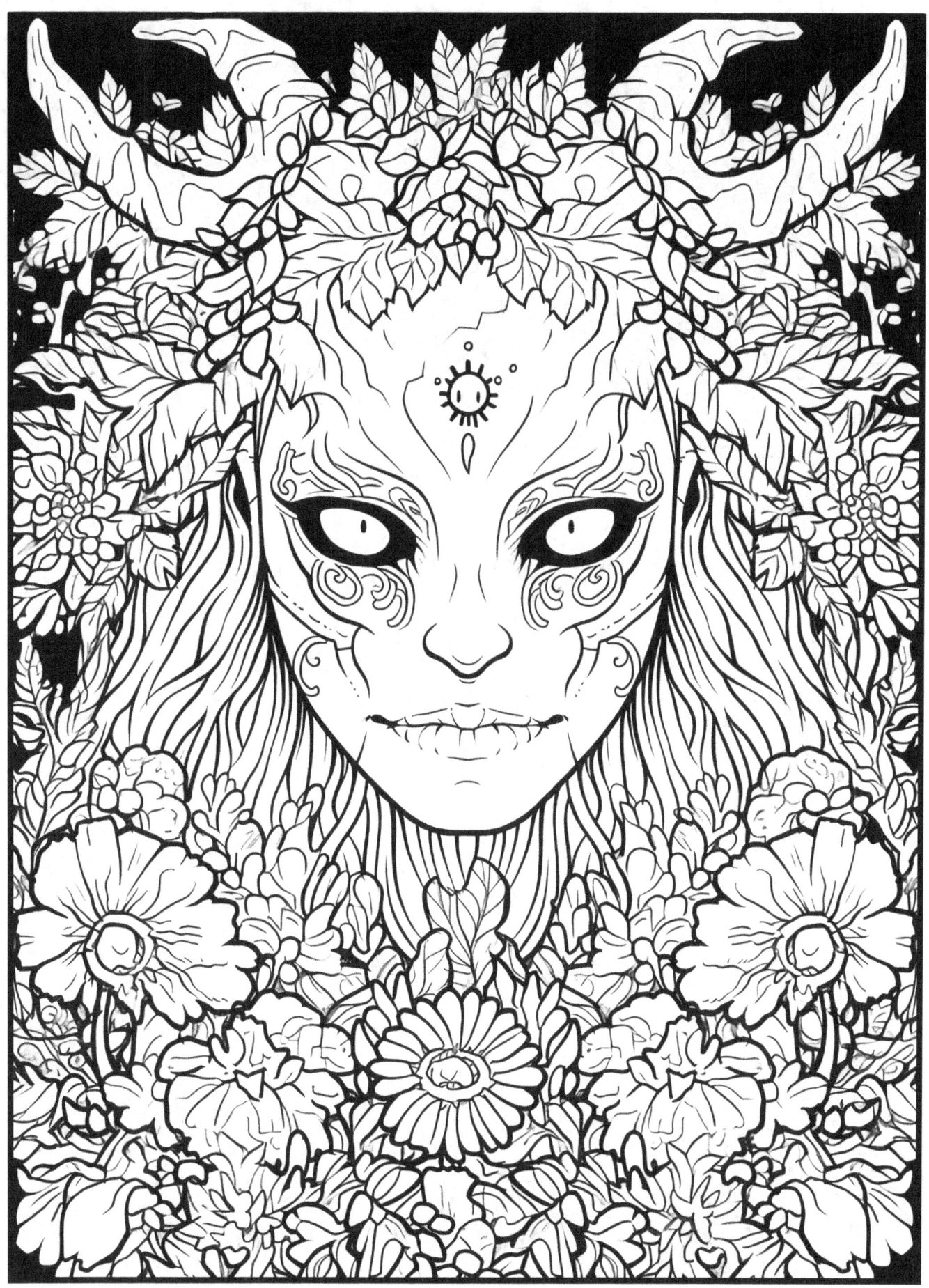

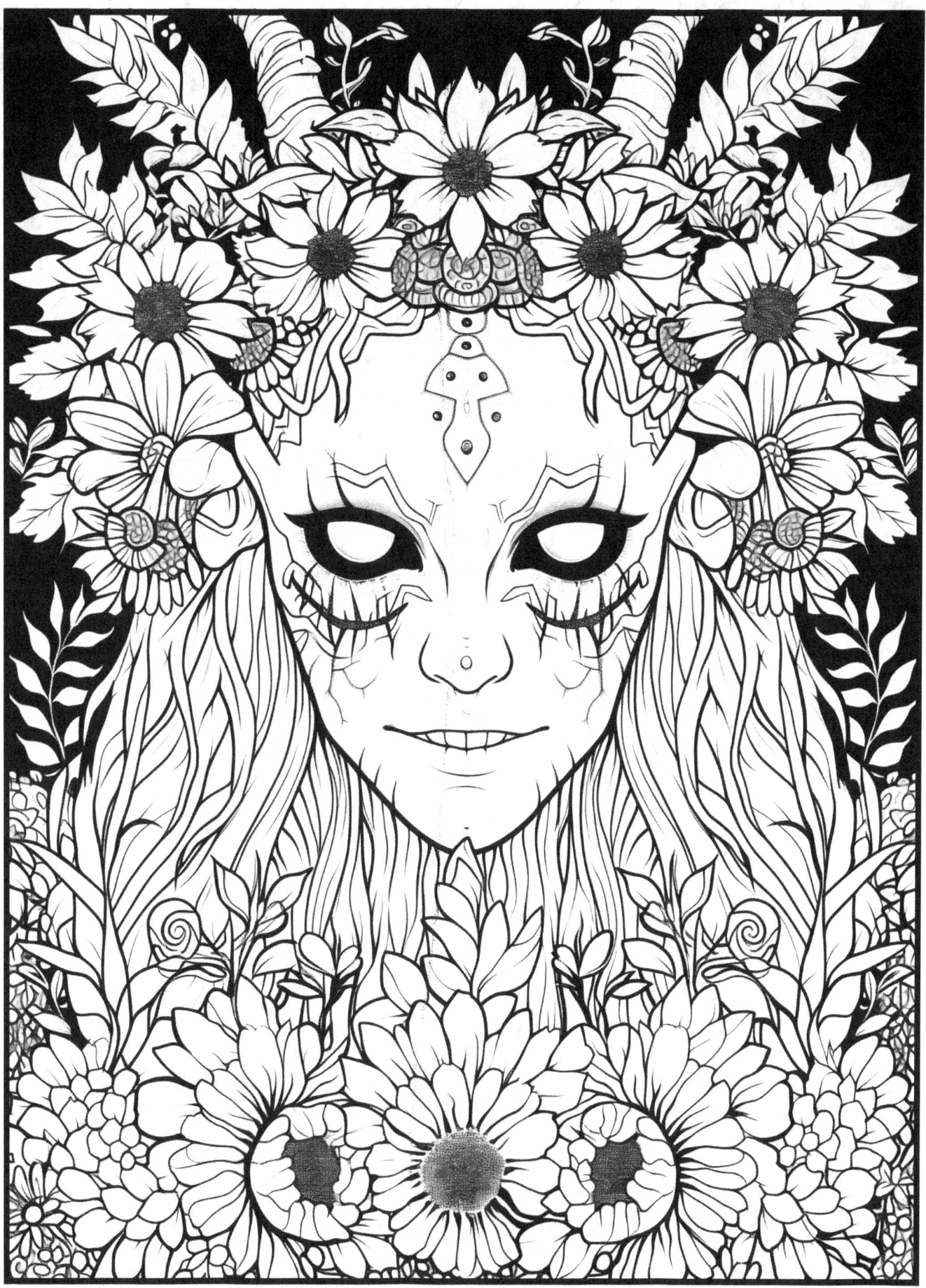

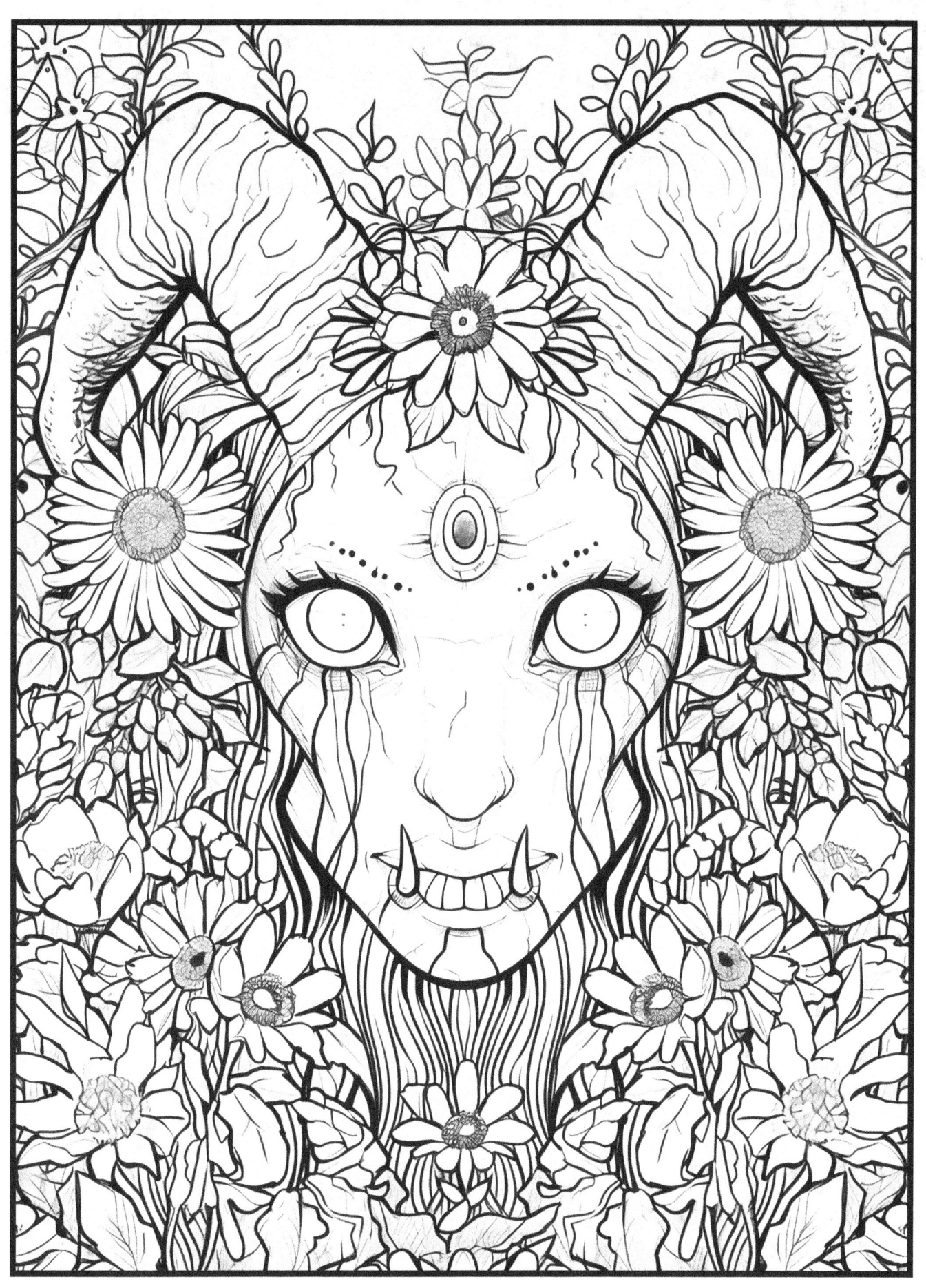

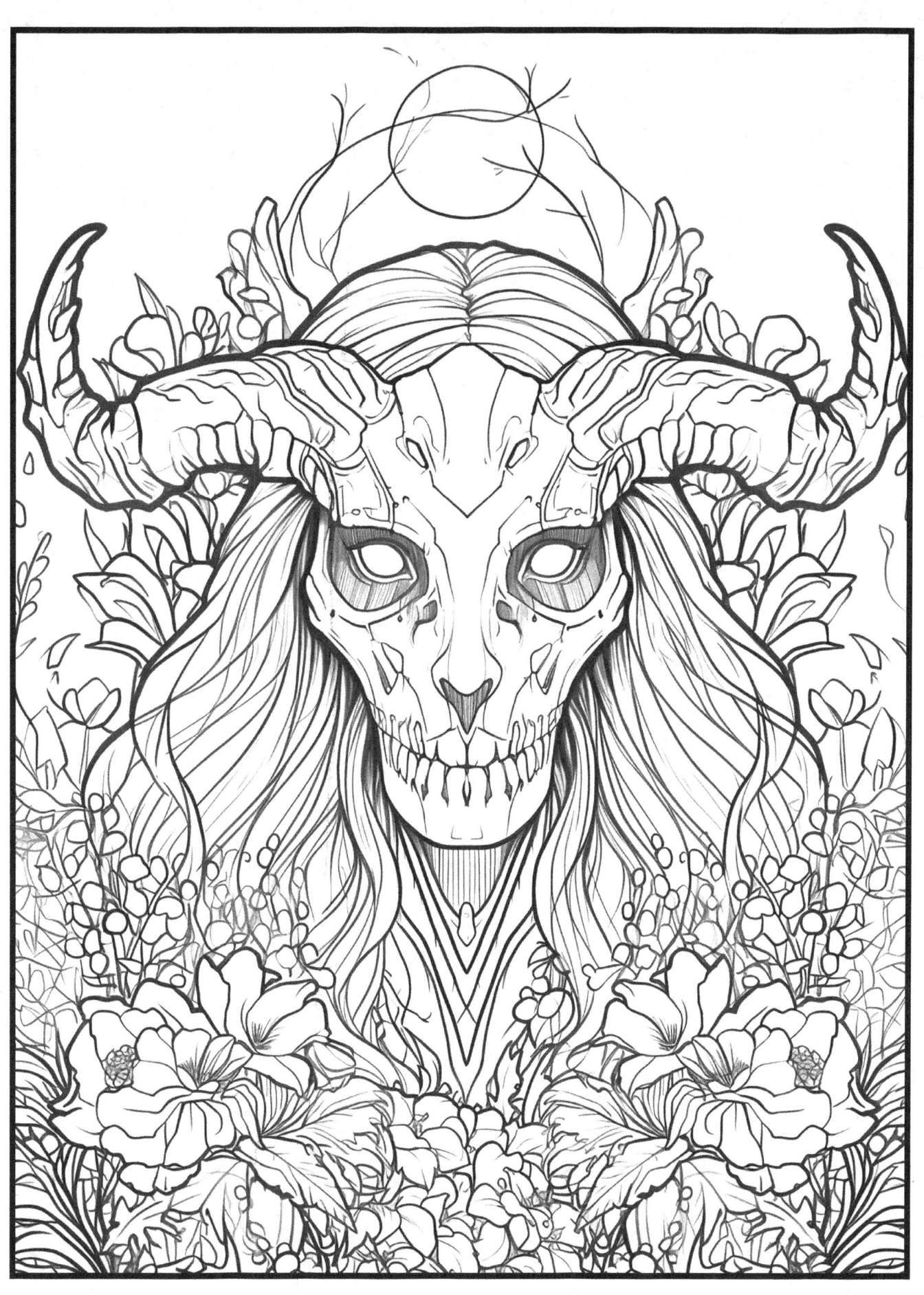

THANK YOU
FOR PURCHASE IT
IT REALLY MEANS
A LOT TO US !

PLEASE SHARE YOUR EXPERIENCE ON THE AMAZON!!!

We hope you have an amazing coloring journey with this book, and we appreciate your feedback to help us develop and deliver more amazing drawings to our audience, and to assist future purchasers in making confident choices.

Scan me !

www.ingramcontent.com/pod-product-compliance
Lightning Source LLC
Chambersburg PA
CBHW080103010626
45794CB00014B/3054